Thanx for the
Cable :)

Your friend
Jordan Marler

EPIDEMIC

EPIDEMIC

✦

Obesity Harassment Bullying

JORDAN NINKOVICH
A Survivor's Story

iUniverse, Inc.

New York Lincoln Shanghai

EPIDEMIC
Obesity Harassment Bullying

iUniverse books may be ordered through booksellers or by contacting:

iUniverse
2021 Pine Lake Road, Suite 100
Lincoln, NE 68512
www.iuniverse.com
1-800-Authors (1-800-288-4677)

ISBN-13: 978-0-595-37963-7 (pbk)
ISBN-13: 978-0-595-67586-9 (cloth)
ISBN-13: 978-0-595-82331-4 (ebk)
ISBN-10: 0-595-37963-X (pbk)
ISBN-10: 0-595-67586-7 (cloth)
ISBN-10: 0-595-82331-9 (ebk)

Printed in the United States of America

Contents

A LETTER FROM THE AUTHOR

I want to thank you and congratulate you for purchasing my book, *"EPIDEMIC."* You have taken your first step in making your dreams become reality. This is not just another fitness book—there are many of them published already. This book is unique because the main focus and desire is to help eliminate the epidemic of obesity, bullying and harassment that is hurting and holding back our youth from developing their full potential. Our children are our future and they will face all the challenges life has to offer better if they are fit, healthy and mentally prepared.

I have enjoyed writing this book and sharing the story of my childhood, the experiences I have gone through and the techniques I have used to help myself achieve my own personal goals. I want to help kids all around the world develop the will power and mind power to conquer the dilemmas and negativity that is holding them back from fulfilling their personal dreams and goals and leading them to a satisfying and joyous life. My mission is to shine hope in their eyes and help teach them that dreams do come true…**all you have to do is believe in yourself.**

It's the difficult times that you are going through that we share together. During these times it is vitally important to be close to your family and friends. They can be your coaches and the best cheerleaders you'll ever have. This is why I have dedicated this book to my parents for always believing in me and always being there for me during the best and worst of times. Thanks Dad, thanks Mom.

"So this is where your journey begins. I will show you the path to your personal success…it's up to you to walk it.

—*Jordan Ninkovich*

1

....our greatest glory is not in ever falling but in rising every time we fall...

—Confucius

Journal Entry 13
February 13, 1998

Stumbling, I quickly headed to the bathroom of the east wing of the school. Locking the door behind me and panting from shortness of breath I leaned over the sink. Drums pounded in my head to the rhythm of my heartbeat and as my eyes slowly closed I grasped the small container. I wildly gasped for air and my eyes shot open as I heard the tormenting chants from my classmates begin to get louder and louder. They found me!

Their chants continued to get louder and their taunting voices were ringing in my ears. "Come on fatty get out of there!" "He probably can't because he's too fat!" Breathing heavily from fear, beads of sweat began dripping to the rhythm of the leaking faucet, drip, drip, drip. Terrified, I felt as though I was shrinking and being drawn into the walls around me. Frantically, I popped the lid off the container and the round, white objects spilled onto the counter top scattering away from me like tiny mints.

*The echoing chants die down and eventually stop giving my tormentors a chance to catch their breath. I look down, feeling dizzy. I see the red lid of the container staring back at me from the floor which seems unstable from my shaking legs. The chanting starts again and this time it's louder, so much louder, and a deafening sensation takes over my hearing and I feel like I am underwater, drowning in a sea of words. My sweaty hand slips off the counter turning my attention to the container. As I rub the sweat from my eyes letters begin to form on the bottle spelling out the word **PAINKILLER.** As I slowly lift my head and look into the mirror the image staring painfully back at me was pale and withdrawn. I could feel my eyes starting to burn as they exploded into uncontrollable crying.*

The chanting escalates as I cup my hand into the water while reaching to scoop up the scattered pills on the counter top. Heavy pounding begins at the door. They're coming in! Dropping the pills I slowly turn around and face the enemy at the door. I'm cold with fear not knowing who or how many were going to come crashing through. The chanting stops along with my heart. The door flies opens...It's my parents???? I quickly look around. I'm at home in my own bathroom. How can this be? I slowly begin to realize the chants were those in my mind being replayed from a situation that had occurred at school earlier on that week.

Without hesitation my shocked and bewildered parents hugged and comforted me while trying to make sense of the state I was in. Without answering them and too embarrassed to confide in them I began to realize that this fear could not continue, that I would not let it destroy my life and that I needed help to overcome it. That night as I lay pondering the episode that had just taken place I decided to take a stand; not against the people that hurt me, but a stand to change the path of my life forever.

People say things happen for a reason and I believe what happened to me was for a very profound reason. I suffered just like millions of you today are suffering from an enemy that was robbing me of my self-esteem and the ability to enjoy all that life has to offer. The enemy came with a name: it was called obesity, harassment and bullying.

Growing up should be a time of innocence, a time of infinite possibility, overwhelming curiosity and above all fun. Everyone, regardless of who they are, where they come from or how they look, is entitled to the best that life has to offer. Unfortunately, we don't live in a perfect world. Threats come in from all sides. A myriad of social problems plague our society and our youth are often the hardest hit. I know this because not so long ago I was a kid and I had a problem.

I was the "fat kid" in class. You know the one. There's at least one of us in every classroom. For me it was at elementary school where I first learned my place. I was always the biggest kid in class, usually the tallest and definitely the widest. When I was really young I felt healthy, happy and full of life but it wasn't long before the other kids let me know just what I was. The fat kid, blubber butt, tubby, chubby, wide load, and on and on it goes. I was always the center of attention, center stage, under the spotlight so to speak. But I was no comedian. I was the joke.

I love basketball. Everyday I would practice my shot. I wanted to be the best shooter in the school but one thing was in my way, I was too fat. It was hard. I remember playing at lunch and trying out for the teams. Being picked last was hard but being benched was even harder. What hurt the most was the teasing and bullying I got not just from the crowd, but also from my own team members. I was being laughed at for just trying to play the game I loved. I was laughed at because I turned red and then purple in the face from shortness of breath while I was trying to run up and down the court. I jiggled and they giggled! This really hurt a lot. Through all this, the love for the game never left my heart but the negativity I experienced poisoned it, leaving me without a flicker of light or hope of becoming what I wanted to be. I hid behind my shyness while I cried inside praying for an answer to escape the torment.

My conditioning came in the form of teasing, harassment, humiliation and bullying. Embarrassment was like my right arm, it was just part of me. I would usually force myself to swallow all the teasing. I would try to let it roll off my back, hopefully to get swept away under some carpet somewhere never to be seen again. Out of sight, out of mind. Unfortunately that stuff sticks and wouldn't you know it, it becomes part of you too. Days turned into weeks, weeks turned into months, months into years and years turned me into a scared, confused teenager with a self-image the size of a peanut. Still I tried to brush it off but often things such as this go from bad to worse. As I grew into a teenager so did my tormentors. They became quicker, harder and more ruthless with every passing grade. Elementary school kids can be hurtful and mean. Junior High school kids can be insensitive and cruel. But High School kids can be malicious and evil.

I remember countless nights of crying myself to sleep. Sounds like a cliché but there's a reason for that. I felt alone. School was a nightmare. My social life was non-existent. I was picked last for every team. No girl would come near me. Any dream of love or having a relationship with someone became a nightmare. I felt lonely and empty inside thinking that the only arrow cupid would strike me with would be a cursed one. Feeling like this was just as bad as being teased. Why didn't people find me attractive, I would ask myself? Fat people can love too! I realized though that T.V. and advertising firms have brainwashed everyone into thinking that if you don't look like a movie star or a model, you're not attractive. In other words, we are conditioned to believe that it is our outward appearance that attracts people to us while forgetting what is really important and that is what is inside us that really counts. Don't get me wrong, yes looks are important, but looks come and go, from young to old, but what is inside that person, their character, their personality, and strengths are what will be with that person forever. Believing this I said, "one day the right girl will find me and see me for who I really am." So I decided to put girls aside for now because I had other things to worry about!

I was afraid to take off my shirt when we went swimming for fear that someone would see me jiggle. I would eat lunch alone so no one would stare and laugh. I was a prisoner inside a prison of fat, guarded by bullies who would point, laugh and harass me endlessly. I avoided as many situations as possible that would inevitably end in embarrassment. Unfortunately, unless I was going to lock myself in a room somewhere and throw away the key, the humiliation would have to continue. When things were at their worst, I thought about ending it all. I entertained these thoughts but quickly realized that **this was not an option**. It never is for anyone in any situation. It's the easy way out. The selfish way. The cowardly way.

Unfortunately there has become a very dark and destructive option that more and more of our youth turn to—drugs and alcohol. Drugs and alcohol are Predators which hunt out and find young kids and adults who suffer from depression, low self-esteem, anger and obesity. I was the perfect candidate, the perfect recruit. I was weak and wounded from everything I had endured over the years and the Predators tricked me into believing that they could help the pain and solve the problems I faced. At first it seemed that way. Heck, I thought the Predators were pretty cool. Life looked better and I was forgetting the pain. The problem was I was beginning to forget myself, who I was and what I stood for. Did these Predators begin to change my life? **YES**, but not in a good way. They were beginning to drag me down a very dark path. Fortunately for me I quickly noticed that this dark path was not an option for me and hopefully should never be for anyone. I am so thankful that I decided not to follow that path and I hope that if you are in that dark place now, you will grab my hand and let me lift you into the same light that so clearly lit the way for me.

I told myself my obesity and the subsequent life crippling effects associated with it would have to be endured. There would be no hiding from them. I would just have to live with it. Or would I?

In high school just like many students, I began to look at my world and question it. Why was I the way I was? Who was to blame? What could I do about it? As we all know, there are thousands of factors at work shaping a human being. Our upbringing, social forces, genetics and our own mental state are but a few. Overeating and weight gain in turn is the result of many factors as well. Low self-esteem, inactivity, social pressures, boredom, habit and simple enjoyment of eating are a few. The fast food industry plays a huge role as does advertising and the media who spread their message. Never before has the Western World been more programmed to consume. Society wants it fast, good and cheap. "Would you like to super size that?" is a question that has brought with it scale-shattering consequences.

USA Obesity Rates Reach Epidemic Proportions

- 58 Million people are overweight, 40 Million are classified obese and 3 Million morbidly obese

- 8 out of 10 people over the age of 25 are overweight

- 78% of Americans are not meeting basic activity level recommendations

- 25% are completely sedentary

- There has been a 76% increase in Type II diabetes in adults 30-40 yrs old since 1990

Obesity Related Diseases

- 80% of Type II diabetes is related to obesity

- 70% of cardiovascular disease is related to obesity

- 42% of breast and colon cancer is diagnosed among obese individuals

- 30% of gall bladder surgery is related to obesity

- 26% of obese people have high blood pressure

Childhood Obesity Running Out of Control

- 4% of children were overweight in 1982 | 16% were overweight in 1994

- 25% of all white children were overweight in 2001

- 33% of African American and Hispanic children were overweight in 2001

- Hospital costs associated with childhood obesity rose from $35 Million (1979) to $127 Million (1999)

Childhood Obesity Running Out of Control

- New studies suggest that one in four overweight children already show early signs of Type II diabetes (impaired glucose intolerance)

- 60% already have one risk factor for heart disease

Surge in Childhood Diabetes

- Between 8%–45% of newly diagnosed cases of childhood diabetes are Type II and are associated with obesity.

- Whereas 4% of Childhood diabetes was Type II in 1990, that number has now risen to approximately 20%

- Depending on the age group (Type II is most frequent in the 10-19 year age group) and the racial/ethnic mix of group stated

- Of children diagnosed with Type II diabetes, 85% are obese

This is an epidemic of catastrophic proportions and lack of exercise and poor food choices are to blame. We all learn best at a young age and early on our brains become programmed to eat whatever it is that we desire. There is no denying that burgers, pizza, chicken wings and chocolate bars taste pretty darn good. Unfortunately our bodies, when looked at as machines, function poorly on these types of fuel. Greasy, high fat, carbo-hydrate loaded diets pack on fat. It's as simple as that. Like an overloaded car, our bodies store fat to the point where it is impossible to perform to optimum levels and because of this the health risks as we have seen can be devastating.

There is another factor at work that is often disguised to be our ally in the fight against fat. Perhaps the only thing that is put in our faces more than this doctrine of mass consumption is the quick and easy solutions to battle weight gain. We've all seen them on television. Infomercials filled with beautiful models that tell you "you too could look like this" if you use their "revolutionary product" for just 15 minutes a day. It's just not realistic. It takes more than a wheel on a stick, an elastic band, miracle pills or dancing. Most of these products are geared up to attack our insecurities and do little or nothing to attack our fat. Some can be helpful but most have the sole purpose of making their creators money. That's the bottom line. It's true that diets can work, exercise fads and products can work but the only way to truly fight the problem and get results is to change your way of thinking and in essence, change your life. Have no doubt about it, this can be very hard but the simple fact is the rewards are indescribable and the life altering benefits are worth the hard work. The hardest thing about any endeavor is how to start. People are often afraid to embark on a journey for fear of failure. **There is no failure as long as you give it a shot**. You'll never know until you begin.

One thing I want to get clear is that this program is not for everyone. There are many people out there who are perfectly happy with the way they are and I'm all for that. The only thing I'm saying is that excessive weight can be extremely unhealthy both physically and mentally. This book is for people who do want to make a change and for those who seek hope in overcoming the bullying, harassment and teasing that they endure by learning new skills that can be used toward accomplishing any goal or desire you wish for your life. This book is for those who do want to look and feel better about themselves. **Health and happiness is our goal and that's the bottom line.**

There are thousands of analogies that sum up life and how we should live it. The same principles run through most of them but they can be very useful. The one that I remember most is quite simple but it puts things into perspective nonetheless. Imagine you are standing on the edge of a cliff. This is your life. Basically you have two choices, (1) you can stay on top of the cliff, never moving forward and forever waiting, or (2) you can take that leap of faith and fly. Unfortunately too many people choose the first option. They never take a chance, never change and are unhappy as a result. The second choice is by far the hardest one because at first we don't know how to fly. Fortunately we can learn how to fly and when we're ready we can take the leap. This sounds cheesy but it's true.

After grade 10, I decided that I had waited on the edge of that cliff long enough. I was going to jump off and see what happened. One night, laying in bed it came to me. I decided to make the change. Starting on the last day of school, my goal was to go from 270lbs to 200lbs over the summer break (3 ½ months). It was a goal I wanted to achieve. I was determined I was going to do it. I knew it wouldn't be easy but I knew with hard work and dedication I could do it. Three and one-half months later on the morning of the first day of school I weighed myself in at 198lbs. I had a feeling that cannot be described. I felt as though the smile on my face would never come off. When I walked into school, everyone thought I was a new student. For the first time in my life I held my head high. I became the basketball player I always wanted to be. I became one of the hottest 3-point shooters around. Finally my eyes shone with hope, strength, passion and love. I became more social and more interactive with everyone. I was high on life and I felt invincible. My grades went from failing to through the roof! My outlook on life was so positive that no words can describe it. I was ready for anything. I could take on the world and nothing could put me down now. I knew my life would never be the same. It felt like I could do and be anything I wanted to be. I loved life! I had a new life. It wasn't just because I looked better. It was because I felt like a different person. I had changed my way of thinking. That feeling transformed my life and I believe that I can help you transform yours. **All you have to do is take that leap and let your dreams become reality!**

WHAT EXACTLY IS BULLYING AND WHAT ARE THE COMMON CHARACTERISTICS OF A BULLY?

No one really knows the answer to the question of why people become bullies. If we knew the answer to that there would be no epidemic. What we do know for sure though is that society, the media and your home life can help to influence and fuel the potential to bring out this anti-social behavior in people. Bullies are not born but created by the environment they live in.

If we take a building for instance that has been built with certain flaws we have the option of tearing it down and rebuilding it from scratch. Unfortunately this is not an option for human beings but the beauty of being human is that we are born with the unique ability to change and better ourselves whenever we have the desire to do so. A bully doesn't have to remain a bully all of his or her life. They have the option and ability to change into caring and productive human beings at will.

I feel sorry for those that are bullied but I feel just as, if not more, sorry for the bully. My own experience of being bullied was horrible and my initial reaction was to want to act out and ultimately hurt that person as much as they had hurt me. No one in their life time should have to experience this but the reality is that it is happening to someone somewhere every day and we have to stop it.

One thing that made my experience painful was watching and listening to people I thought were my friends, laugh and make fun of me. Having only a few friends to begin with made this all the more devastating. For parents out there you must realize that if your child is being bullied your chances of his or her ever telling you about it are slim to none. You must realize that your children will not communicate their feelings to you, either from embarrassment or humiliation, and 90% of the time parents are totally unaware their children are suffering from this problem. There are signs though that you should definitely watch for such as depression, anger, anti-social behavior, overeating, drugs and/or alcohol. These are early indications that there is definitely a problem somewhere that needs to be carefully looked at.

Now in retrospect, I understand and realize that our energy and resources are geared, for the most part, toward looking only at how we can assist those that are bullied. When you think about it, shouldn't we concentrate a little more on how we can help the bully? The key to stopping or at least slowing down this epidemic is to address the reasons why a bully demonstrates this behavior in the first place.

Bullying occurs when an individual intentionally and repeatedly sets out to hurt or harass another person through acts of cruelty. Although most statistics will reveal that the actual act of bullying usually occurs time and time again with the same bully/victim, bullying can also be classified as such with the occurrence of one, single incident.

You have to keep in mind that it is natural for kids to call each other names, joke about one another or engage in horsing around without it being classified as bullying. The difference is when the people involved are not usually friends and when one is trying to enforce power over the other. This usually happens when the bully is bigger, stronger and able to intimidate people easily or exclude them from a group.

Bullies and their victims are at high risk for developing a wide range of problems if the cycle is not broken and they are not given the treatment and support needed. They can show signs of the following:

Bullies:

- Aggression, delinquency, academic problems, internalizing problems, anxiety, negative peer reputation and problems throughout adulthood

Victims:

- Withdrawn behavior, reputation as someone who is weak and able to be bullied, school problems, poor concentration, anxiety and quitting school because of fear.

It is imperative that parents, schools and society become active participants in addressing this problem of bullying and harassment and realize that changes must be made at home, in the classroom, and on the play ground.

Inside the pages of this book I want to reveal to you the power, the techniques, the motivation and the inspiration you already possess to help those that experience in their lives the terrible effects of being bullied and harassed. Even though you may not know it, feel it or believe it, YOU have the POWER hiding somewhere deep inside you to rise up and conquer this evil epidemic. So let's do it.

There are three types of bullying: physical, verbal and the detrimental affects of gossip. These three powerhouses are destroying the youth of tomorrow the same way it almost destroyed me.

Physical	Psychological	
	Verbal	Social
Hitting Kicking Punching Pushing/shoving Stealing	Insults Name-calling Threats Comments about how someone looks or talks Comments about someone's ethnicity (culture, color or religion)	Gossiping Rumors Ignoring Not including someone in group activities
Results		
Can hurt a child's body, damage belongings (clothes, toys, etc) or make a child feel badly about himself or herself.	Can make a child feel badly about himself or herself.	Can make a child feel alone and not part of the group.

April 24, 2001 (National Institutes of Health)

Bullying Widespread in U.S. Schools, Survey Finds:

- Bullying is widespread in American schools, with more than 16 percent of U.S. school children saying they had been bullied by other students during the current term, according to a survey funded by the National Institute of Child Health and Human Development (NICHD).

- The study appears in the April 25, 2001, Journal of the American Medical Association. Overall, 10 percent of children said they had been bullied by other students, but had not bullied others. Another 6 percent said that they had both been bullied themselves and had bullied other children. Another 13 percent of students said they had bullied other students, but had not been bullied themselves.

- "Being bullied is not just an unpleasant rite of passage through childhood," said Duane Alexander, M.D., director of the NICHD. "It's a public health problem that merits attention. People who were bullied as children are more likely to suffer from depression and low self esteem, well into adulthood, and the bullies themselves are more likely to engage in criminal behavior later in life."

- The NICHD researchers surveyed 15,686 students in grades six-through-10, in public, parochial, and other private schools throughout the U.S. The nationally representative survey was part of the U.S. contribution to the World Health Organization's Health Behavior in School Children survey, an international effort in which many countries surveyed school-age children on a broad spectrum of health-related behaviors.

- For this study, researchers defined bullying as a type of behavior intended to harm or disturb the victim, explained the study's first author, Tonja R. Nansel, Ph.D. This behavior occurs repeatedly over time and involves an imbalance of power, with the more powerful person or group attacking the less powerful one, Dr. Nansel added. Bullying may be physical, involving hitting or otherwise attacking the other person; verbal, involving name-calling or threats; or psychological, involving spreading rumors or excluding a person.

- The children were asked to complete a questionnaire during a class period that asked how often they either bullied other students, or were the target of bullying behavior. A total of 10.6 percent of the children replied that they had "sometimes" bullied other children, a response category defined as "moderate" bullying. An additional 8.8 percent said they had bullied others once a week or more, defined as "frequent "bullying. Similarly, 8.5 percent said they had been targets of moderate bullying, and 8.4 percent said they were bullied frequently.

- Out of all the students, 13 percent said they had engaged in moderate or frequent bullying of others, while 10.6 percent said they had been bullied either moderately or frequently. Some students-6.3 percent-had both bullied others and been bullied themselves. In all, 29 percent of the students who responded to the survey had been involved in some aspect of bullying, either as a bully, as the target of bullying, or both.

- Bullying occurred most frequently in sixth through eighth grade, with little variation between urban, suburban, town, and rural areas; suburban youth were 2-3 percent less likely to bully others. Males were both more likely to bully others and more likely to be victims of bullying than were females. In addition, males were more likely to say they had been bullied physically (being hit, slapped, or pushed), while females more frequently said they were bullied verbally and psychologically (through sexual comments or rumors).

- Regarding verbal bullying, bullies were less likely to make derogatory statements about other students' religion or race. "There seem to be stronger social norms against making these kinds of statements than against belittling someone about their appearance or behavior," Dr. Nansel said.

- Both bullies and those on the receiving end of bullying were more likely to have difficulty adjusting to their environment both socially and psychologically. Students who were bullied reported having greater difficulty making friends and poorer relationships with their classmates. They were also much more likely than other students to report feelings of loneliness.

- "It's likely that kids who are socially isolated and have trouble making friends are more likely to be targets of bullying," Dr. Nansel said. "In turn, other kids may avoid children who are bullied, for fear of being bullied themselves."

- The study authors also reported that bullies were more likely to be involved in other problem behaviors, such as smoking and drinking alcohol, and to do more poorly academically. However, youth who were both bullies and recipients of bullying tended to fare the most poorly of all, experiencing social isolation, as well as doing poorly in school and engaging in problem behaviors, like smoking and drinking.

- "Unfortunately, we don't know much about this group," Dr. Nansel said. "We need to learn more about them to provide them with the help they need." She added that it is not known whether these children are first bullied by others and then imitate the bullying behavior they experienced, or if they are bullies who were later retaliated against.

- The study's authors concluded that the prevalence of bullying in U.S. schools suggests a need for more research to understand, and devise ways to intervene against, bullying. The authors noted that researchers in Norway and England have shown that school intervention programs can be successful. These programs focused on increasing awareness of bullying, increasing teacher and parent supervision, establishing clear rules prohibiting bullying, and providing support and protection for those bullied.

The NICHD is part of the National Institutes of Health, the biomedical research arm of the federal government. The Institute sponsors research on development before and after birth; maternal, child, and family health; reproductive biology and population issues; and medical rehabilitation. NICHD publications, as well as information about the Institute, are available from the NICHD Web site, http://www.nichd.nih.gov, or from the NICHD Information Resource Center, 1-800-370-2943; e-mail NICHDInformationResource-Center@mail.nih.gov.

2

….we are what we repeatedly do. Excellence therefore is not an act but a habit

—*Aristotle*

Journal Entry 12
Dec.10, 1997

Loneliness hit a new low today. It started off like every other lunch hour of my pathetic high school life, eating alone. Not just that but being watched, like I were some caged animal or the main attraction in a freak show. Why do they point and laugh like they've never seen someone eat before?

Things were going normally or at least normally for me, until a classmate of mine came up to me and said, "Yo, Jordan, you want the rest of these fries?" I was in such shock that this guy was even talking to me that I didn't know what to say but "yes." When you're used to being exiled during lunch in a high school everyday, and someone out of the blue offers you some food, it's like a hot girl running up and kissing you for no reason, it just doesn't happen! So I looked at these fries and still feeling a little hungry I began to enjoy them.

I thought to myself, hey, maybe this guy noticed me for the right reasons. Maybe this time things will be different. I looked for and found the classmate later that day to thank him. Instead, he thanked me for his laugh of the day and soon after I found out why.

The fries I ate that lunch hour were fries collected off the ground.

As we go through life, no matter who we are, where we're from or what we do, we all must face and overcome obstacles (e.g. bullying, harassment, teasing). I like to look at these barriers as doors that are thrown up in my path. They come in from all over the place and can pop up out of nowhere. You can be moving along just fine then WHAM! A door gets thrown up in your face. These doors can be made of paper, wood or solid steel. They can be made of pure negativity. They can be made up of fear. They can be made up of forms of bullying, harassment and teasing. They pretty much can be made up of anything. Simply put, they are the obstacles that stand between you and the positive, happy life you desire.

More often than not these doors are easily opened because we have the keys readily available. We are able to unlock most doors and pass through them with little effort. Unfortunately, some obstacles are not so easily overcome and sometimes the keys are hard to find. They are stored somewhere in the nooks and crannies of our minds. Some keys can be found and used at a moments notice but many are hidden and can take time to locate. We might even come up against a door that seems impossible to open, like the times I was getting bullied and teased. It felt like a door I could never open, until now. Search as we might we cannot find the key. In these situations we must pick the lock. Still, sometimes your lock pick doesn't work. The door still won't open. What then? Then you break down the door using sheer will. You kick it in. Knock it down. Run right through it. Lean on it until it collapses. Do whatever it takes but don't let anything hold you back. Your mind holds all the keys to all that stands in your way. It's in your mind that you will find the key to unlock the power, to stop all bullying, harassment and teasing that taunts you and to move you forward to accomplish every goal you have for your life.

There are three main phases in this program. In turn, each phase has a number of steps. They are as follows:

- **PHASE 1—THE MIND**

  - **Step 1—From Negative to Positive Thinking**

- **Step 2—Goal Setting**
- **Step 3—Visualization and Meditation**
- **PHASE 2—THE BODY** (Chapters 3-6)
- **PHASE 3—CONCLUSION**

PHASE 1—THE MIND

I believe that the human mind is the most powerful, mysterious and valuable substance on the planet. The brain is capable of astounding achievements and can take us to levels never before imagined. You need only look at the world around you to realize the extent of its reaching. Science, medicine, technology and human compassion are all the result of the complex human mind. Inversely, you only need to pick up a newspaper or turn on the television to witness the negative side of the connotation. War, discrimination, hate and apathy are also inventions spawned from the human mind. The mind is a fragile substance and therefore must be treated with care and respect.

Stop for a moment and think about this: we do absolutely nothing without thinking about it first. The mind holds all of the keys that will unlock all of the doors on our journey. This is by far the most important part of the program. It all begins with re-programming your mind to think in ways that are beneficial to you and your body. It is within your mind that the first phase of your transformation will take place. It is in your mind that you will find the power to overcome your tormentors and to accomplish your goals.

When I made the decision to change my life, I started out by first taking a negative and turning it into a positive. Yes, I was overweight. Yes, I was miserable. Yes, I felt alone. Yes, I was getting bullied and teased but, yes I could make a change. That was my motivating factor. I began to believe that it was possible for something good to happen. I started to believe in hope. The thing about hope is that unless you can predict the future, there is always hope, for everyone. There is always a chance that tomorrow can be better than today. It all comes down to how you perceive your life because when you look at it, you really have only two choices. You can look at things positively or you can look at things negatively. Of course there are millions of variations and differing degrees of positives and nega- tives in between but cut and dried there are really only two choices. I know you're probably thinking, wow, a breakthrough! The power of positive thinking! Why didn't I think of that?" It sounds like a cliché and once again there is a reason for that. It has been tested and it works. Everyone knows that positive thinking can help us achieve almost anything but very few actually put it into practice and use it as a tool to change their own lives. Few people know how to use positive thinking and make it work for them. Many believe that negative thinking is just something they must live with and endure. Unfortunately, negative thoughts can manifest them- selves in depression and a negative self-image. In turn, depression and low self-esteem often bring with them inactivity and increased eating or even thoughts of ending it all or feeling that you're not getting anywhere in life. I'm not saying get rid of all negative thoughts and everything will be okay. There will always be some negatives in life. I'm saying that you must take the negatives and turn them into positives. Often we hear of how writers, poets and artists use the pain in their lives, or in the world around them, to create their best work. I know this to be true. The same applies here. Take whatever suffering that you feel inside and turn it around. You feel bad that you are overweight. You feel bad that you're getting bullied. You feel bad that people tease you. You feel lost and alone. Use these feelings as motivators. Transform them into something useful. Begin to believe that a good change can take place.

Human beings are creatures of habit and conditioning. Throughout life, people become programmed to believe certain things, do certain things and behave in certain ways. It is extremely difficult to break out of a routine or habit once it has been conditioned into our very being. The first step in Phase 1 is to be aware of negativity and the effect it has on you and to learn to concentrate only on thinking positive thoughts. This isn't easy. True, there are a lot of horrible things going on in the world right now and bad things can happen to anyone at any time. People get sad, people get sick and people die. This is a simple fact of life so shouldn't it also be true that wonderful things can also happen to anyone at any time? There is still and always will be a lot of great people and good things in this world. People can become happy, people can heal and people can turn their lives around and truly live. Whatever reality you create for yourself is the one you must live with. If you want to enjoy your time on earth, try to make it the best reality possible. All you have to do is try and keep trying no matter what. It is time for you not to let negativity control you anymore! I'm going to show you the way to believe in yourself.

There are essentially five steps used to recondition our minds. They are positive thinking, goal setting, visualization, affirmation and meditation.

STEP 1—Negative Thinking to Positive Thinking

Negativity. The characteristics of the word negativity are: contradiction, destruction, disagreement, begrudging, opposition, pessimism, uncooperativeness, unenthusiastic, unresponsiveness and unwillingness.

These are just a few forms of negativity that people display when you let it take control of your life. If you take the time to look around you and observe people in a crowd you will find it easy to identify those who display negative behaviors. There are so many negative influences bombarding us daily that it is easier than you might imagine to fall prey to this adverse behavior pattern. You don't need to be overweight or teased or even bullied to suffer from this. Whether young or old, people are letting down their defenses and welcoming negativity into their lives with open arms. When you let negativity into your life you are at risk of developing low self-esteem, insecurity, depression and more.

What is self-esteem? Very simply put, it is having pride and confidence in yourself. The feelings and thoughts you have about yourself, whether positive or negative, affects your self-image and your attitude toward life.

An echoing chant that has been heard throughout the playgrounds of schools and hallways everywhere at one time or another is *"sticks and stones may break my bones, but words will never hurt me."* A lie hides quietly in this chant and unfortunately I found out the hard way. I would take a broken bone over cruel words any day. Broken bones can be healed but hurtful words can linger in the shadows of your mind forever. The truth is words can shape us, hurt and torment us and most definitely define us. Today's youth are particularly susceptible to other people's opinions, especially those of their friends and classmates at school. No matter how well parents may think they have provided the skills for their children to overcome adverse situations they often fall short when they are tested. As parents, your chances of even hearing from your child that they are facing situations they can't handle is very unlikely. No teenager wants to admit, especially to their parents, that they can't take care of themselves. This is why it is crucial that we put a stop to this epidemic by supplying our youth with ways to strengthen their self-esteem and self-image so that they will have the confidence to take on the cruelty that lies within the playground and hallways of our schools.

Following is a chart showing examples of how parents, teachers, grandparents or anyone else that is influential in the lives of our children can choose to build up or tear down their self-esteem.

BUILDING A HEALTY SELF-ESTEEM	CAUSES OF LOW SELF-ESTEEM
Parents can help their children to develop a healthy self-esteem by:	Experiences that can encourage a low self-esteem:
• giving praise when deserved	• criticism and words harshly spoken
• listening respectfully to our children	• being hit, beaten and yelled at
• encouraging our children to share their experiences with you	• being teased and laughed at
	• being ignored by people
• giving lots of hugs and encouragement	• having few or no friends
• share your child's success in school, sports or other activities that they are interested in.	• trying to reach someone else's expectations of how you should look, speak and act
• know their friends and help them to build trustworthy relationships.	• doing poorly in school or outside activities

From this moment forward, the words *"I can't"*, *"too hard"* and *"I hate"* will leave your vocabulary. They will leave your internal vocabulary and external vocabulary. While you're at it, get rid of all the negative words that run through your head. They are baggage and you don't need them. Of course no one can be 100% positive 100% of the time. That's impossible. What is possible is to make a conscious effort not to use negative words and phrases and try to think positive in all situations. At first this might seem futile and extremely difficult. It will be. At first it might not seem to work at all. You might even think that it is stupid and hopeless. Once again these are the results of a negative self-image. You might be so used to looking at things negatively that turning things around seems strange and unnatural. Creating a positive self-image is tough. It could take hours, days, months or years to create a positive outlook. Here are some further examples of a positive vocabulary. Add your own if you can think of some.

I can	I'm happy	I'm motivated	I'm successful
I will	I'm excited	I'm strong	I'm a good person
I am	I'm special	I'm not afraid	I'll decide
I see	I can win	I will continue	I won't give up
I feel good	I will win	I won't falter	I'll keep going
I feel great	I have overcome	I have moved forward	I'll stay strong
I look good	I won't stop	I will press on	Live

Our society is trained to want results immediately. If it doesn't come fast and easy we don't want it. That's the mistake. To truly see results you must persevere, fight and never give up…ever. Remember, old habits die hard. They like to stick around and mess things up for as long as possible. Only by reprogramming your mind can you get rid of them. Think positive and continue to think positive. Let the negative thoughts run their course but always try to combat them with something positive. Start making the effort to use positive phrases. *"I can," "I will," "I won't stop,"* are a few. Also use your positive attitude in your mind. Over time, just by changing your vocabulary and your inner voice, you will begin to feel better. Other people will notice too. Make no mistake, there will still be negativity. It is still all around us. Just when you think you are making progress, something or someone will try to knock you down or hold you back. An iron door will somehow find its way right up in front of your face. Make the choice to face it and conquer it in a positive way. **Begin to forget what you would do and start doing what you should do!** The negative alternative is no longer an option. With these methods you will learn to block the negative messages

STEP 2—Goal Setting

The next step in your transformation is to make a goal. Goals will be the starting and ending points on your road to success. They are something to strive for and they are something to keep you moving forward. I believe that a major problem with our society is an overwhelming lack of goals for people in general. We must have something that pushes us forward or we stagnate. People dig themselves into holes that seem to be impossible to get out of. Whether you want to lose weight, learn how to play the guitar, or run a marathon, it all begins with a goal. Goals should always be challenging but also realistic. Goals are very important especially when you are being harassed, bullied and teased like I was. It is important for anyone who gets treated like that to use these methods to help build a stronger self-esteem and block out the negativity you might be facing. Building a positive outlook on life helps you to strive for success in anything you want to accomplish. Getting rid of extra pounds is realistic. The great thing about weight loss is that regardless of who you are, where you're from or what you look like, you can always lose weight. That is a biological fact. You can change your diet and more often than not, you can exercise. You can change your way of thinking. You just have to make it a goal. Once again it's going to be hard. The younger you are the easier it will be. Start by writing down your ultimate goal, and then you can break it down. My ultimate goal was to go from 270 lbs to 200 lbs over the course of a summer. As an ultimate goal this was fine but I had to first break it up into sub-goals. For example I first wrote down the goal of going from 270 lbs to 250 lbs and went to work. When I reached 250 lbs…mission accomplished…SUCCESS. **ANY SUCCESS IS STILL SUCCESS!** Remember if your goal is not reached in a certain amount of time or if you actually rebound back to where you were, or worse yet you get heavier, don't look at it as a failure. Actually you can't fail because failure is no longer part of your vocabulary therefore it's not an option. As long as you have a goal and you continue to work hard, the results will come. I would say I guarantee it but in life there are no guarantees. In the end it's up to you to reach your goal.

Some Points to help you set effective goals:

- **Express your goals in a positive manner**. *"I have", "I am"* and *"I believe"* should become the building blocks of any goal you want to achieve.

- **Be precise about your goal**. Try to set a realistic goal to achieve. Your goals should not be too easy or too hard so that they become unrealistic. Have a clear and realistic understanding of what you are trying to achieve.

- **Make sure you write your goals down** so that you can refer to them at any time in case you need that extra boost of encouragement.

- **Take one big goal** (such as losing a certain amount of weight, or getting conditioned to run a marathon) **and break it down into smaller goals**. If a goal is too large, then it can seem at times that you are not making progress toward it. By keeping your goals small you will be able to reward yourself on each success and soon you will be on your way to reaching the final goal.

- **Set specific and realistic goals.** Don't let other people set unrealistic goals for you. You know best your desires and ambitions.

- **Have no fear of failure.** Failure is not in your vocabulary. Every step forward is a success. If you are afraid to fail you will not take the risks needed to move ahead.

- **Be prepared to work hard.** To achieve anything of real worth you must be prepared to dedicate your time and effort toward that achievement.

STEP 3—Visualization

Everyone at one time or another has fantasized about being someone else, being in an unbelievable situation or having an amazing fulfilling life. Most people have dreamt of flying, pictured themselves rich and famous or at least thought about having some kind of amazing power. This is quite natural and can be used as an escape or a release. By using our imagination we can transform ourselves and transport ourselves into any situation or circumstance that can be conjured up. Unfortunately the same does not hold true for real life. There are techniques, however, that we can incorporate into our lives that can have similar effects. Visualization techniques have been around for a long time. They can be used to help us in almost any facet of life. Professional athletes can use them when not in play to stay sharp, students can use them before a big exam, they can be used to help alleviate stress and of course to help you lose weight. By simply visualizing yourself as having lost weight, you can reprogram your mind to help you get there. It sounds crazy but it works. First you need to stand in front of a mirror and look at yourself. Take a good long look because the person that you see will have changed drastically within a few weeks or months. Now, close your eyes and slowly begin to clear your mind until all pictures are gone and all you see is an empty box. Now picture yourself standing in front of that mirror again and begin to look deeply past the reflection of the mirror imagining what you want to look like. Continue visualizing your new image until you see it looking back at you. At first this may not be easy but don't get discouraged. Keep concentrating on that new image and once that magical image appears, study it and embrace it. You may feel a warming sensation or a jolt of happiness and this is normal so enjoy that wonderful feeling. Think positive and relax. Take long deep breaths and continue to visualize the person you wish to become. See yourself standing in front of that same mirror once you have accomplished your goal of looking like your new self image. Lock the new image of yourself into your mind and remember it. You should be able to refer back to it at any time. Visualizing the positive and meditating on that positive image plays a major role in helping us reach our goals. By seeing ourselves in a new light, our minds begin to change and work in positive ways. (*"Seeing yourself successful, helps you feel and act successful therefore making you become successful."*). If you want to be successful and lose weight or have the strength to overcome bullying or harassment you first have to lock that belief in your mind. By making the decision to do this you can create a self-fulfilling prophecy.

Now that you have begun to think positive, determined your goals and visualized your new self, it's time to develop a permanent, positive attitude that will be the backbone for success in helping you to overcome your tormentors. You will gain the willpower, self-esteem and strength to fight off the negativity that haunts you in order for you to achieve your goals.

These three steps, used together will help reprogram your mind so that it is ready to transform your body and unlock your hidden potential. The next challenge is to combine the three steps in such a way as to change your cognitive functioning on a subconscious level. In order to do this, you must eat, drink and sleep a positive attitude. You must constantly chase your goals and you must visualize yourself reaching those goals and becoming the person you want to be. You will gain the strength to do anything you desire.

STEP 4—Affirmation Training

I want you to make yourself 9 affirmation cards about the size of a baseball or recipe card. You can add as many as you need. These will be your Affirmation Cards and will be the culmination of the three steps we discussed above. On each card you will:

1. **Write** a positive message

2. **Make** a realistic goal

3. **Declare** a visualization statement that you can see in your mind. How would you feel after reaching your goal? That's your visualization statement.

You know that voice you hear in your head? Well you also have another one. It's called your sub-conscience. Your sub-conscience is a hidden voice or recording that plays over and over again and contributes immensely to the way you act and look at life. So, if you program your self-conscience with the techniques I am showing you, you will become happier and have a more positive outlook on life instead of a negative one. Keep this in mind while practicing these new techniques. Look at any new challenge as if you have already accomplished it, "see and feel yourself doing it!" and speak to yourself as if you have already done it. E.g. "I have completed my workout today and I feel great" or "I blocked out the teasing with my positive attitude, I feel happy." Even though you might not have done those things that day you will visualize yourself accomplishing these things a lot faster and easier when you think you have already completed them.

AFFIRMATION CARD EXAMPLE:

> ### 1. I am strong and determined!
>
> ### 2. I have lost 25 lbs - I feel alive!
>
> ### 3. I am happy, healthy and full of positive thoughts. Nothing gets me down!

Read your affirmation cards out loud before you go to bed and when you wake up in the morning. This will help you reprogram your subconscious by becoming the first and last thing in your mind before and after sleep. A good idea is to place your cards near your toothbrush so you won't forget to read them in the evening and in the morning when you get up. It will probably feel strange at first but who cares. Feeling strange is a small price to pay so keep doing it. Keep your affirmation cards up to date. After completing a goal, make a new card or use an old card to maintain that goal. Begin to memorize your cards. Read them with your eyes closed. Relax, breathe deeply, meditate on your goals and visualize your new self-image. Repeat the messages until you actually begin to see what you are saying. Then you will begin to believe and only then will you be ready to make the change and become what you have seen.

STEP 5—How to Relax, Meditate and Visualize your goal.

In order to become one with yourself and visualize yourself completing your goals in life, I need to first teach you how to meditate and relax so that you can visualize and see your new self image properly. Meditation and relaxation can be used in everyday situations by relaxing and calming you while preparing you for anything. This is what you need to do. First, I want you to find a quiet, comfortable room where you will not be distracted. If possible, dim the lights to create a more relaxing mood. Next, sit comfortably and have your affirmation cards with you that outline your goal, positive statement and visualization statements. Start reading your card out loud to yourself until you feel confident you have it memorized. Next, I want you to close your eyes and begin to take long, deep breaths. Feel your muscles and mind begin to relax. I want you to begin to clear your mind from all troublesome thoughts and worries. Continue breathing with a steady rhythm in through your nose, hold it for 3 seconds, and exhale through your mouth. With your eyes closed, start to visualize an empty pyramid/triangle. It may take some time before you can clearly see the pyramid/triangle but if you continue to breathe in, breathe out, deep and steady and concentrate only on seeing that pyramid, you will.

Begin to picture the words **"DEEPER"**, going up the left side of the Pyramid all the way to the top. Now visualize the words, **"RELAX"**, going down the right side of the pyramid to the bottom.

I want you to concentrate on your breathing while visualizing the Pyramid. When taking a deep breath visualize the word **"DEEPER"** going up the Pyramid and when exhaling, see the words **"RELAX"** going down the Pyramid.

By visualizing the Pyramid and the words it helps you to practice your visualization skills but it also helps your body to relax. Continue this process until your body feels weightless and at ease. Continue the breathing and now visualize the goal you want to achieve in the "middle" of the empty Pyramid/triangle. Keep your breathing rhythmic and start to concentrate on that goal or new self-image in the middle of the Pyramid. When you feel ready begin to see your new self image and start to say out loud your memorized affirmation statement, e.g. "I enjoy life." "My self-esteem is growing stronger each day." "I believe in myself". "I am physically fit and in shape" etc." Keep repeating your affirmation statement and visualize it until you see a crystal-clear image of what you want to achieve or until you are completely satisfied.

JOURNAL WRITING

Journal writing and charting achievements is a key aspect in completing your goals and improving yourself by helping you understand life's situations and why things happen the way they do.

Since the dawn of time, mankind has been charting his achievements, events and goals. From drawing illustrations on cave walls to the history books we read today, mankind has used these methods with great success. Writing and charting your achievements while walking the path to success will help strengthen your skills by seeing and understanding why things happen and what you can do about it. We both know that the kind of negative situations that occur to us due to harassment, obesity and being bullied are ones that we like to keep to ourselves and have trouble seeking the appropriate guidance for because we feel they are too painful or embarrassing to share.

Writing daily situations that occur, whether hurtful or pleasant, help us open up and express those situations that we otherwise would keep to ourselves. By writing these experiences down, we can learn to counteract them with a positive attitude and with positive goals.

It is important to try and share your hidden feelings and negative situations with your family and close friends. I know you might feel embarrassed or scared, (I was too,) but by writing down the positive and negative situations that have happened to you, you will begin to see the situation more clearly and gain strength to confront the problem. By doing this you will find the understanding, courage and confidence to eventually freely express yourself to your family, close friend or mentor.

Make or buy yourself a daily journal so you can chart your success. My personal journal was divided into four categories; Negativity, Positive Attitude, Goal and Image. When a negative situation occurred during the day, I would write it down in the "negative" column and automatically counteract the situation with a positive reaction in the "positive attitude" column. Next, taking the positive reaction I would create a "positive goal" that could be used to help me prevent that negative situation from happening to me again in the future. Finally, create your "positive goal image" and <u>see yourself</u> preventing that negative situation with an "image statement" in the image column.

Together with your positive thinking, goal setting, visualization meditation and affirmation training, you will have created a new attitude. Armed with this new attitude you are ready to take the next step in the transformation of your life. From now on you have the mind power to accomplish anything in life with these methods, but most importantly, from here on you are not going to let anyone or anything put you down. **"Now raise that head up and let's walk this path to success!"**

3

....it is hard to fail, but it is worse never to have tried to succeed

—Theodore Roosevelt

Journal Entry 11
Nov. 17, 1997

All right! A field trip!!

When you're in school and the teacher says you're going on a field trip, it's almost like Christmas morning. It feels great! Hell, anything is good just as long as you get out of school work and that damn class room. Well, at least that's what I thought until I heard we were going swimming.

This is the last place an overweight kid like me wants to be. It's bad enough that I'm trying to hide myself under clothing, now I've got nothing to hide under but the water line. So we get to the pool and I make sure I'm far enough away in the corner of the changing room so nobody can see me. I have a choice to make. Either I go out in the pool with a shirt on or a shirt off. For me this was a major decision. Kids of normal weight don't even think of these things they just suit up, jump in and have a great time. I was thinking to myself that I would probably attract more attention with a shirt on because they would probably think I was too dumb to take it off or something like that, so I decided to go without one. So out I went. "Oh no everyone, here comes the tidal wave," someone yells. Well no sooner had he said that than I have the whole pool looking my way wondering why the hell there would be a tidal wave in an indoor pool. Then, they saw me. Their laughs echoed across the water like stones skipping across the lake. While I slowly turned red like a lobster that just got boiled, I slithered into the pool. Hiding my figure under water I tried to enjoy the swim but the taunting remarks just kept coming.

I wasn't having much fun so I decided to get out of the pool early. As I was climbing out of the pool I slipped and fell to the floor and a crackling rip echoed across the pool as I hit the floor. Well, the moon came out early that day. My bathing suit ripped…life's great.

(Before starting any diet or exercise program please consult your physician.)

When it comes to dieting what you eat contributes a lot to you completing your goals for getting in shape. To change your diet, which we will get to soon, takes a lot of willpower and self-esteem, which is exactly what you started developing in Chapter Two. Not being able to do this is not an option. You will be excited and motivated by your new, heightened sense of self-esteem and this will give you the willpower to change your diet. It will be difficult but you don't look at it in that way anymore. It is a challenge, which you are **successfully** going to complete.

Nevertheless, I too was where you are not too long ago. I remember the days of enjoying a cheeseburger without hesitation, making an ice cream cone or eating a chocolate bar whenever I wanted one. I would storm through the cupboards in the kitchen in search of goodies to satisfy my sweet tooth and the cravings. I was there—those were tasty days! But like both of us, deep down inside we knew that something had to change but we didn't know what until now.

"Don't let junk food control you—YOU CONTROL IT!" You can't let these type of foods control your life. Don't let them be that important to you. Ask yourself these questions, "Do I really need to eat this?", "Is this helping me to achieve my goals?" "Is this doing my body any good?" What junk food does for you is give you an uncontrollable craving that tries to control your life. BUT NOT FOR LONG! Now that you realize how to program your mind we need to use this program to get you in control of these cravings. It will be hard some days, especially the days when people have been cruel to you. Days that are full of teasing and harassment are the days you will feel so down on yourself that it will be easy for you to let junk food control you.

I remember days like that, being in class and being bullied and teased. It seemed that no matter what I was being teased about everything seemed to revolve around me, but unfortunately, in a negative way. When I got bullied and teased I automatically looked to junk food and sweets to help sweeten me up and make me feel better. Junk food helped give me that feeling of satisfaction and that everything was okay but that feeling only blinded the real truth and the real truth was that things were not okay. So, together we are no longer going to experience days like that. Those days are gone forever. Instead of being down and letting junk food control your thoughts and emotions, the best thing to do is to conjure up those feelings of sadness and anger and let those feeling feed your motivation to succeed and reach your new goals. Don't let those people put you down. Let their taunts and comments roll off your back. Keep that head up high and tell yourself that what they are saying is not true and remind yourself deep down inside that soon things will be different. Visualize your new self-image. By doing this you will fuel your **motivation** instead of fueling yourself with junk food and anger.

Now that you have reprogrammed your mindset, have a more positive outlook on life, and have seen your new self-image, it's time to work on your new diet. Most diet programs out there tell you that you need to stop eating junk food and eat healthier. They are right but it's not that simple. Why most diets out there fail is because most people don't think positive and they either go into withdrawal over the lack of junk food in their diet or they lose interest and sooner or later they are right back eating junk food again. In order to change your diet, it is very important to **remember that "you are what you eat!"** and by changing your diet you are one step closer to becoming what you want to be.

First things first. I want you to stop eating junk and fatty foods, but not right away. In order for your body not to go into withdrawal the best thing to do is to gradually wean yourself off the bad foods you eat. By doing this you not only wean yourself off junk food but you build stronger willpower. This means, for example, that if you drink two cans of soft drinks everyday, start by cutting back to one pop a day for the first week. From there on have one pop three or four days a week until the craving for soft drinks starts to diminish. Your goal will be to cut your consumption of soft drinks to one day per week. Save that one special day a week for pop or junk food. This is true for all types of junk foods. The only way to get rid of the cravings is to use your positive mind and the willpower that you are developing and wean yourself off the junk food day by day, week by week until you don't desire it anymore. Remember, use the one-day-a-week rule. On one special day a week you can have one snack and one meal from your junk food menu. Look at it as a reward for working so hard on your diet and goals. You deserve one special day a week and this is your reward but you have to work hard to receive it and enjoy it.

When I say junk food, these are some of the foods I want you to wean yourself from and eventually stop eating.

- all types of fast foods

- deep fried foods

- pop/soft drinks

- sugar/candies

- chocolate

- potato chips

- french fries

- cheese

- butter

- pizza/pasta (if you must have pasta—only whole-wheat pasta)

I'm not saying don't eat these foods ever again, I'm asking you to gradually wean yourself off them if you eat these foods a lot. Save them for that special day once a week to enjoy. The key to enjoying foods like the ones above is to take control over them and you decide when you will eat them and if they are worth compromising your goal for. You will notice an increase of natural energy and your body will feel more "alive" just from cutting back on the foods listed above.

These are the types of foods I want you to fill your kitchen with and start eating on your new diet. Replace the foods listed above with these nutritious and vitamin power packed foods. **Your body will love you for it!**

- breads (only whole grain wheat, high-fiber breads—stay away from white bread)

- brown rice

- potatoes (baked) or sweet potatoes

- all types of fruits

- all types of vegetables

- skinless chicken breast

- lean beef and steaks

- tuna fish, salmon (all types of seafood)

- oatmeal

- no-fat, low-fat yogurts

- low-fat, no-fat granola bars, rice cakes

- salad with low fat dressing

- eggs, egg-whites

- when preparing meals use good oils e.g. extra-virgin olive, flaxseed, etc.

- watch butter and other spreads you would put on bread or your meal. (Use low-fat spreads)

Refer to the *"New Healthy Kitchen Menus"* in Chapter 3.

These are just some types of healthy foods you need to start eating. These are mostly meal-type foods so for snacks during the day refer to *"Your New Snack Menu"* in Chapter 3.

Don't be shy about eating. **Not eating is NOT good**. The best thing to do is to at least have something to eat every two to three hours if you can. It keeps your metabolism up and helps you maintain a good appetite. Portion size is important. Try having five to six smaller meals a day or having something every three hours. The size of your open hand should be the portion size of your meals. Don't ignore your hunger or skip meals. When eating or snacking every two to three hours remember to fill yourself up with healthy foods. Don't eat and stuff yourself with the empty calories found in junk food.

When it comes to breakfast, lunch and dinner, breakfast should be the biggest meal of your day. By far it is the most important meal to keep your mind and your body functioning at peak performance. While sleeping at night your body burns off calories and uses energy to rejuvenate itself so you feel rested in the morning. After doing your affirmation cards in the morning have a well rounded breakfast to refuel your body and jumpstart your mind for the day. A good healthy breakfast should include a balance of protein and carbs from a healthy source of food. Remember don't go overboard on the portion size of your meals. Following are five breakfast options for you to use as examples. Try all five and if you find one that you really like, just stick to it. This rule applies to the upcoming meals as well. Also, you can include a fruit serving with whatever breakfast you pick e.g. fruit cup, banana, orange, apple etc. For a beverage drink lots of water. Skip the fruit juice once in a while or have a glass of skim milk but remember **the most important beverage you can have throughout the day is WATER**. Water keeps you hydrated and helps to flush all the toxins out of your body.

Many dieters won't drink water because they fear it will lead to water retention. The opposite is actually the case. What appears to be fat on overweight people is often retained water. When the body gets less water it senses this and holds on to every drop. Yet, studies show when we drink enough water the body eliminates excess fluids. When your body is breaking down fat you need even more water to help eliminate the extra waste that is produced.

BREAKFAST OPTIONS

#1

Bowl of Oatmeal. Mix oatmeal with 1.2 c. skim milk or water. Add berries or raisins or have your fruit on the side.

#2

Scrambled egg with whole-wheat toast. Two farm fresh eggs or mini egg white carton. Mix with skim milk and scramble. Two slices of whole-wheat toast spread lightly with jam. Top your eggs with ketchup or salsa.

#3

Pour a bowl of high fiber (e.g. raisin bran, mini wheat) cereal with fruit. Pour a bowl of cereal w/skim milk, add fruit or have it on the side.

#4

Enjoy low or no fat yogurt with a whole-wheat English muffin. Add fruit to yogurt or have on the side. Lightly jam the whole-wheat muffin.

#5

French toast. Two slices of whole-wheat toast served with low or no fat syrup with fruit on the side.

These are just some breakfast ideas that you should consider having in the morning. Experiment with different combinations to see what suits your lifestyle and your personal taste best. Breakfast is not for everyone. You may be in a hurry or late for school or work so try and fit in the best breakfast you can by using some of these examples from your new diet plan. Remember, you are allowed to snack every two to three hours in between meals so refer to the snack menu to remind you what you can have.

When it comes to lunchtime, the portion should not be as big as breakfast because you should already have had some kind of snack in between breakfast and lunch. If you miss your snack do not add this to your lunch.

It is not good to super size your meals. Below I am listing five lunch meal options you can have. Remember these are guidelines and you can experiment to find out what you like best.

NOTE: (Before each meal, try and drink 1-2 glasses of water. Water tends to fill up the abdominal space and make you feel full faster.)

LUNCH OPTIONS:

#1
Enjoy a whole-wheat tuna sandwich. Two slices of whole wheat or high fiber bread, one can of light tuna packed in water. You can use low-fat or no-fat mayonnaise or spread. Add fruit if desired.

#2
Lean lunch (turkey, chicken etc.) meat sandwich with veggies. Two slices of whole wheat or high fiber bread. Add lunchmeat, lettuce, cucumber, tomatoes, pickles etc. Add mustard or any healthy spread. Enjoy some veggies (carrots, broccoli, celery stick etc.) with low-fat dip.

#3
Healthy low-fat meal replacement bar.

#4
Tuna/chicken salad with chopped fruit. Chop up some fresh iceberg or spinach and add 1 can of tuna or pre-cooked chicken and some mixed berries. Toss altogether with a low-fat dressing and enjoy!

#5
Protein/meal replacement shake. Add some fresh fruit if desired. Mix with water or skim milk.

NOTE: Use these options as a guideline. Try other things but stick to your New Healthy Kitchen Menu.

Once again, the five options above are a guideline to help show you examples of what kind of meals you should be having. Use the breakfast, lunch, and dinner guidelines to help you get more meal ideas from your New Healthy Kitchen Menu.

During midday, between lunch and dinner, you can enjoy a snack if desired. (Make sure the snack size is a half portion size.)

There are some things that you need to know about dinner. When it comes to dinner and with it being the last meal of your day, the time you eat plays a very important role in what and how much you eat. If you are an early diner (5:00p to 7:00p) then create a healthy dinner from your New Kitchen Menu and use the correct portion size. Eat slowly making sure you savor the flavor of each bite. If you are a late diner (7:30p to 9:00p) then you need to watch how much you eat. As it gets later in the evening, your body tends to slow down and shift into a more relaxed and resting state enhancing the possibility that you will want to go to sleep right after eating. When you go to bed on a full stomach your body starts digesting your food at a slower rate meaning your metabolism also slows down so your body tends to not burn off as many calories as if you were awake. Therefore your body will store more fat.

Below are five dinner options you can try. Remember, you can experiment with any of these options or create your own!

DINNER OPTIONS

#1

Chicken Stir Fry—Use 4 to 6 ounces of boneless, skinless chicken breast and any vegetable combinations you like (e.g. carrots, snap peas, red pepper, tomatoes, celery, mushrooms, broccoli, etc.). Add some soy or teriyaki sauce and serve with 3.4 to 1 cup of brown rice.

#2

Steak and vegetables—Use a lean, six-ounce steak with a medley of vegetables. You can use either fresh or frozen.

#3

Chicken/beef or shrimp with whole grain pasta—Cook 6 ounces of lean chicken, steak or a hand full of pre-cooked shrimp and add it to your cooked whole-wheat pasta. You can also add some veggies to your pasta as well. Mix together with a marinara sauce.

#4

Grilled/baked fish filet with baked potato—Bake or grill a 6-ounce piece of fish (salmon, tuna, swordfish, halibut etc) with a medium size potato. Add salsa or any "light" spread to your potato.

#5

Grilled/baked chicken with salad—Grill or bake a 6 ounce, skinless, boneless piece of chicken. Enjoy with a tossed salad sprinkled with a light vinaigrette.

YOUR NEW HEALTHY KITCHEN MENU FOOD GUIDE

BEVERAGES:

- Skim milk or 2% milk

- Soy Milk

- Lots of water

- Tomato or V-8 juice

- Natural juices

- Protein shakes

- Meal replacement shakes

Note: You can have your soft drink **only** on that **one Special Day** that you have picked. Don't keep your soft drinks in the fridge so you won't be tempted to have them.—**(Out of sight, out of mind!)**

FRUITS:	MEATS	VEGETABLES
• Peaches	• Lean Roast beef	• Broccoli
• Pears	• Skinless chicken	• Carrots
• Pineapple	• Cornish Hen	• Cauliflower
• Cantaloupe	• Turkey	• Asparagus
• Watermelon	• Stir fry beef	• Peas
• Strawberries	• Lean Steaks	• Sweet Potatoes
• Blueberries	• Salmon	• Potato (Baked)
• Raspberries	• Tuna (no oil)	• Beans, green
• Cranberries	• Swordfish	• Onions
• Oranges	• Halibut	• String beans
• Nectarines	• Shrimp	• Mushrooms
• Grapes	• Snapper	• Zucchini
• Apples	• Cod	• Pickles, dill
• Honeydew Melon	• Crab	• Lettuce
• Papaya	• Crayfish	• Brussel sprouts
• Mangos	• Sole	• Cabbage
• Bananas	• Lean lunch meats	• Cucumbers
• Grapefruit		• Radish
• Kiwi		• Peppers

GRAINS:

- Whole Grain Bread
- Brown Rice
- Oatmeal
- Whole Wheat Flour

- Spaghetti Squash
- Tomato

NEW HEALTHY SNACK GUIDE MENU

These are the types of snacks you can enjoy in between meals. Remember to drink lots of water throughout the day to keep you hydrated and help fill you up faster.

SNACKS	FRUITS:
• Protein Shake	• Peaches
• Healthy Smoothie	• Nectarines
• Glass of 2% milk	• Plums
• Yogurt—no fat/low fat	• Apricots
• Handful of nuts	• Watermelon
• Rice Cakes	• Apples
• Beef jerky	• Oranges
• Tuna fish (water)	• Grapes
• Low fat granola bar	• All types of melon
• Low fat crackers	• Bananas
• Whole wheat toast/jam	• Strawberries, raspberries
• Air popped popcorn	• Pineapple
• Gelatin, sugar-free, 1 cup	• Papaya

Vegetables:	**Fruits:**
• Carrot sticks	• Blackberries
• Celery sticks	• Grapefruit
• Broccoli	• Cantaloupe
• Cauliflower	• Passion Fruit
• Peppers	• Pears
• Mushrooms	• Mangos
• Tomatoes	• Banana
• Lettuce	

Note: You can use a low fat dip or vinaigrette for your fruits and veggies.

YOUR "JUNK FOOD" MENU

These are the types of junk food I want you to start cutting back on and eventually eliminate completely from your diet. For that **one special day a week**, you can enjoy **1 snack and 1 meal** from the list below. This is your reward for your hard work!

REMEMBER: DON'T LET JUNK FOOD CONTROL YOU—YOU CONTROL IT!

SNACKS:	MEALS:
• Chocolate Bar	• All types of fast food
• M & M's	• McDonalds
• Smarties	• Burger King etc.
• Coffee Crisp	• Chinese food
• Your favorite etc.	• Cream soups
• Milk Shake	• Pizza
• Ice cream	• Pasta
• Popcorn (flavored)	• Hot dogs
• Cookies	• Hamburgers
• Pudding	• Chicken wings
• Pop Tarts	• French fries
• Candy	• Bacon
• Pop	• Cheesecake
• Chips	• Peanut Butter
• Cheesies	• Donuts

CHILDHOOD DIABETES

An epidemic of obesity is sweeping our nation. As one walks through crowded airports or malls, the prevalence of obesity is immediately apparent. In people over 20 years of age, obesity now affects about 33% of the population. In children and adolescents, obesity has increased by almost 50% over the past 20 years and has an estimated prevalence of at least 25%. While genetics plays a role in this trend, it is also likely that increased fast food consumption and a more sedentary lifestyle are contributing factors.

Major complications and risks associated with childhood obesity include psychosocial disturbances, hypertension, hyperlipidemia, respiratory dysfunction, slipped capital femoral epiphyses and diabetes mellitus. As body mass index (BMI, kg/height in m2) increases to values above 27, the risk for developing these complications markedly increases. Consequently, it is essential for pediatricians, family physicians and others who work with youth to identify those who are at risk. With early intervention and management strategies that emphasize exercise, dietary adjustment and behavioral modification, it may be possible to prevent these worrisome complications.

Clinical Diabetes: Type 2 Diabetes Mellitus in Youth: A Growing Challenge
Author/s: James R. Hansen, Michael J. Fulop, Maya K. Hunter
Spring, 2000

Cardiovascular risk status among American youth is getting worse, not better according to Dr. William B. Strong.

A case in point is the growing problem of type 2 diabetes among adolescents.

It's an issue that physicians "haven't been very aware of. It was thought to be primarily an adult disease. It's not an adult disease any longer. This is a real disease that is increasing by leaps and bounds in the pediatric population," declared Dr. Strong, director of the Georgia Prevention Institute and chief of pediatric cardiology at the Medical College of Georgia in Augusta.

For example, investigators at Children's Hospital Medical Center of Cincinnati have documented a 10-fold increase in cases of adolescent type 2 diabetes in the greater metropolitan area, growing from 0.7 cases per 100,000 persons per year in 1982 to 7.2 cases per 100,000 persons per year in 1994.

Dr. Strong pointed to a recent editorial by Dr. Stephen R. Daniels, a pediatric cardiologist at Children's of Cincinnati, who observed that not only the prevalence but also the severity of obesity continue to increase among American youth (J.Pediatr. 134(6):665-66.1999).

This is a particularly disturbing development in light of the American Heart Association's 2-year-old declaration that obesity is a major modifiable risk factor for coronary heart disease.

Dr. Russell V. Luepker and his associates at the University of Minnesota, Minneapolis documented that systolic blood pressure measurements increased among Minneapolis 5-8th graders from 1986 to 1996.

"The significance of this increase in blood pressure is the potential for increasing prevalence of hypertension and cardiovascular disease as this generation of children moves into adulthood." (J. Pediatr. 134(6):668 74, 1999.)

Family Practice News, March 15, 2000
Author/s: Bruce Jancin

Using diet, exercise and weight loss, many people can keep their condition in check and prevent serious complications.

Suggestions that you might find helpful:

1. Eat five or six smaller meals a day instead of three big ones.

2. Each day begin to eliminate refined sugar and sugar products from your diet. I know this is not easy but by eliminating just one can of pop a day (full of sugar and caffeine) will start you on your way to a healthier body.

3. Try to avoid too much junk food. Instead enjoy snacks high in Vitamin B and C. These include: strawberries, apples, bananas, cantaloupes, oranges, grapefruit, peaches, pears, kiwi or dried fruit.

4. Enjoy whole grains and vegetables; broccoli, asparagus, cauliflower, radish, mushroom, cucumber, peppers, green or yellow beans, salads. These foods release natural sugars more slowly into the blood stream.

5. Start to exercise regularly. Exercise helps to control your weight and sends oxygen into your tissues and gets your metabolism going. If you are taking insulin now to control your diabetes you should monitor your blood sugar level before exercising and have a healthy snack on hand to enjoy after exercising. As exercise lowers your blood sugar this snack will prevent hypoglycemia.

4

...experience is the child of thought and thought is the child of action...

—*Benjamin Disraeli*

Journal Entry 10
Nov. 14, 1997

I just don't understand why people can't see me for who I am. Everyone is different, that's what makes us unique. I just wish they saw that in me.

I have been playing basketball since grade five; it's all I do, and it's my life. So why do I play something that makes my life hell? I try my best to be enthusiastic and upbeat but no one else sees it and once again the rude remarks are endless. Once, the basketball court was the only place I had to unleash my pain but now I am receiving more every time I step on the court. The crowd distracting you is one thing, but the taunting from your own team mates is another. Every practice and every game I would hear something coming from their mouths like "boom, boom he broke the floor," "big this, big that, fat this, fat that" followed by their nightmarish laughter. It's so distracting. I can't even hear or remember what the coach was trying to tell me to do. I really hate this. I want to quit and my so-called team mates—yah right. It just seems everywhere I go this torment follows me. I feel so alone.

EASY, HEALTHY RECIPES
THE WHOLE FAMILY CAN ENJOY!
(Before starting any diet or exercise program please consult your physician.)

Listed below are just a few recipes for you to try. Be creative about the food you enjoy and substitute healthy fruits and vegetables for the ones you enjoy most. If you are diabetic, look on the Internet under "children with diabetes" for lots of fabulous food choices. Make a cookbook of your own filled with your favorite recipes and surprise your family one day by making them a flavorful, nutritious meal or snack. They will be so impressed!

Curried Chicken Salad with Grapes

3 cups of cooked chicken cut into bite size cubes
1 ½ cups of red or green grapes (whichever is your favorite)
½ cup of sliced celery
½ cup of diced red bell pepper
¾ cup of low fat mayonnaise
2 tbs. of orange juice
1 tsp. curry powder
fresh ground pepper to taste

Directions

Combine the first 5 ingredients in a bowl.
Combine the remaining ingredients in another bowl and whisk together until smooth. Toss the dressing with the salad and serve.

This recipe will serve six people so invite your friends over to help you enjoy this delicious meal!

"I'M GOING BANANAS"—BANANA BREAD

2 cups all purpose flour
2 teaspoons low-sodium baking powder
½ teaspoon baking soda
½ teaspoon cinnamon
1 ½ cups sliced bananas (about 3 ripe bananas)
1 egg
1/3 cup canola oil
2 tablespoons sugar
½ cup unsweetened orange juice
Non-stick cooking spray

Directions

Preheat oven to 350 degrees F. Combine flour, baking powder, baking soda, sugar and cinnamon in a bowl. Stir to blend. In a separate bowl, puree the bananas in a blender or mash well with a fork. Add the bananas and the remaining ingredients to the dry ingredients and mix well. Pour the mixture into a loaf pan that has been sprayed with the nonstick cooking spray. Bake for 40 to 50 minutes. Cool on a wire rack. **ENJOY!**

SMOOTHIES A LA FRUIT

1 cup of orange, passion fruit, apricot, mango (or whatever your favorite juice is)
1 cup fat-free plain yogurt
1 frozen banana
1 cup of frozen strawberries or raspberries
6 packets Equal sweetener or 1 ¾ teaspoon Equal for Recipes or 1.4 cup Equal Spoonful

Directions

Peel and cut banana into large chunks. Place in plastic freezer bag, seal and freeze at least 5 to 6 hours or overnight.

Place all ingredients in blender or food processor. Blend until smooth.

Sit back, relax and enjoy!

SESAME CHICKEN

This chicken is so good it's hard to believe it's been cooked in the oven and not deep-fried.

2 tbsp. Soy sauce
4 boneless, skinless chicken breast halves
3 tbsp. Sesame seeds
2 tbsp. Flour
¼ tsp. salt
¼ tsp. pepper
Butter-flavored non-stick cooking spray

Preheat your oven to 450 degrees. Pour soy sauce into a dish and add chicken coating it with the soy sauce on both sides. In a plastic bag combine the sesame seeds, flour, salt and pepper. Add chicken to the seasoning bag and shake to coat the chicken well. Place chicken in a 13x9 inch-baking dish that has been sprayed with the non-stick cooking spray. Lightly spray the top of the chicken with the butter-flavored cooking spray and bake in the oven for 30-45 minutes or until center of the chicken is no longer pink and the juices run clear. Makes 4 servings. Serve with your choice of vegetables and a small salad.

TURKEY TENDERS JAMAICA STYLE

1 ½ Pound turkey breast, boned & skinned
1 cup of orange juice
¼ cup of lemon juice
¼ tsp. garlic powder
1 tbsp. Jerk seasoning
½ cup apricot preserves

Pierce the turkey breast with a fork several times. Combine orange juice, lemon juice, garlic powder and jerk seasoning in a large plastic bag. Put turkey in the bag, seal and let marinade for at least three hours. If you are cooking these on the BBQ grill you can cook for about 15 minutes on each side. Brush with the preserves on both sides. If desired you can put turkey in tin foil to prevent burning. These can also be cooked in a shallow dish in a 375 degree oven for 30-45 minutes. Serve with a baked potato and vegetables.

QUICK BLENDER MUFFINS

½ cup orange juice
1 peeled orange
1 egg
¼ cup oil
1 ½ cups of flour
¾ cups of sugar
1 tsp. baking powder
1 tsp. baking soda
1 tsp. salt
½ cup raisins or cranberries or blueberries (your favorite)
½ cup of chopped nuts (this is optional)

Cut up your orange and place in a blender along with the orange juice, egg and oil. Blend until smooth. Next add the flour, sugar, baking powder, baking soda and salt. Blend. Add raisins and nuts. Blend just until mixed. Pour mixture into lined muffin tins and bake at 375 degrees for 15 to 20 minutes. Makes 16 large muffins.

VEGETABLE SALAD WITH PASTA

2 cups of broccoli
2 cups of sliced celery
1 cup carrots sliced thin
2 cups cauliflower
2 cups of sliced mushrooms (fresh is best)
2 tbsp. Parsley, chopped
6 ounces of shell, bowtie, elbow or penne pasta (your choice)
1 1/3 cup of low-fat Italian dressing.

Wash and dry your veggie. Place vegetables in a large bowl and cover with the Italian dressing. Refrigerate. Cook pasta until al dente and drain. Toss pasta with the refrigerated vegetables. Add a little salt and pepper to taste.

YUMMY CHICKEN CASSEROLE

3 boneless, skinless chicken breasts cut into bite-size pieces
3 tbsp. of olive oil
¼ tsp pepper
2 cups of broccoli
1—10 ounce can of low-fat cream of chicken soup
½ cup of low-fat mayonnaise
1 tsp. lemon juice
1 tsp. curry powder
½ cup of low-fat cheddar cheese

Sauté your bite-size pieces of chicken that have been sprinkled with pepper slowly over medium heat until the chicken is cooked, approximately 8 minutes. Drain the chicken. Cook the broccoli until crisp and bright green. Drain and arrange in the bottom of a 7-inch casserole dish that has been sprayed with non-stick cooking spray. Place the chicken on top of the broccoli. Mix the soup, mayonnaise and curry powder together and pour over the chicken. Sprinkle cheddar cheese over top of the chicken and bake uncovered in a 375-degree oven for about 35 to 40 minutes. Enjoy with your favorite salad.

SIZZLING SALSA

2 large ripe tomatoes cut in small cubes
1 chopped, medium sweet onion
1 to 2 cloves of fresh minced garlic
6 to 10 small green chilies or 2 to 4 jalapeno peppers. You decide which you like best.

Chop all your vegetables making sure to remove the seeds from chilies if you use them. Combine all ingredients and chill in the refrigerator for at least two hours before serving. Great as a topping for fish, eggs, meat or a dip for crackers.

MEATLOAF

1–11/2 lbs. of lean ground beef
1 beaten egg
1 medium onion, chopped
1 carrot, grated
3 tbsp. ketchup
2 tbsp. worchestershire sauce
2 tbsp. mustard
1 tbsp. hot sauce (Tabasco etc.)
8–10 crushed crackers or
2 slices of bread, (breadcrumbs)

Put all the ingredients in a large bowl and mix well. Place in a 8"x4"x3" loaf pan and bake in a 350 degree oven for 1 hour. Drain any juices from meatloaf and serve with vegetables of your choice and a salad.

GREEN BEANS AND RED PEPPER STIRFRY

1 lb. of green beans, trimmed
1 red pepper, seeded and cut in thin strips
2 tbsp. olive oil
½ tsp. soy sauce
1 tsp. fresh lemon juice

Cook beans in salted water for about 3 minutes. Rinse in cold water and pat dry with paper towel. Heat olive oil in frying pan, add green beans and red pepper and stir fry for about 2 minutes. Remove from the heat and add the soy sauce and lemon juice. Mix and serve.

CANDIED SWEET POTATOES

3 lbs. of sweet potatoes, peeled
1 tbsp. of butter or margarine
4 oz. of maple syrup
¾ tsp. ground ginger
1 tbsp. fresh lemon juice

Preheat oven to 375 degrees and spray a shallow baking dish with non-stick cooking spray. Cut the potatoes in ½ inch slices and cook in boiling water for about 10 minutes. Drain and let cool. Melt butter or margarine in saucepan and add maple syrup. Stir well. Add ginger, stir well and simmer 1 minute then add the lemon juice. Arrange the potato slices in one layer in your baking dish. Overlap the potatoes slightly. Drizzle the maple syrup mixture over the potatoes and bake until tender and glazed, about 35-40 minutes. During the cooking time baste the potatoes with the maple syrup mixture.

AVOCADO, GRAPEFRUIT AND MELON SALAD

1 pink grapefruit
1 yellow grapefruit
1 cantaloupe
2 large, ripe but firm avocados
2 tbsp. lemon juice
2 tbsp. olive oil
1 tbsp. liquid honey
3 tbsp. chopped fresh mint
salt and pepper

Peel the grapefruits, cut into segments leaving the membrane behind and put into a bowl. Cut the cantaloupe in half, remove the seeds and with a melon baller, scoop out the cantaloupe. Add the melon balls to the grapefruit sections and chill for an hour. Next, cut the avocados in half, peel off the skin and cut into small pieces. Toss the avocado pieces with the lemon juice to avoid discoloration of the avocado. Whisk the oil and lemon juice together. Stir in the honey, chopped mint and salt and pepper to taste. Pour dressing over the chilled fruit and enjoy.

PRAWNS, ASPARAGUS AND FRIED RICE

3 tbsp. olive oil
6–8 stalks of asparagus cut diagonally into one inch pieces
½ lb. of button mushroom
12 oz. cooked brown rice
1 tsp. grated fresh ginger root or ½ tsp. of ginger powder
½ lb. of cooked, peeled and de-veined prawns
4 oz. canned water chestnuts drained and sliced
3 tbsp. soy sauce
pepper to taste

Heat olive oil in a wok over high heat. Add asparagus and mushrooms and stir-fry for 3-4 minutes. Stir in cooked rice until heated through. Add cooked prawns and stir-fry for about 1 minute. Add the water chestnuts and soy sauce. Stir-fry for another minute. Season pepper and serve.

RICE PILAF WITH NUTS

1 tbsp. butter or margarine
1 onion finely chopped
12 oz. long grain brown rice
½ tsp. lemon rind
16 oz. chicken stock
16 oz. water
¼ tsp. sale
4 green onions finely chopped
2 tbsp. fresh lemon juice
¼ cup of pecan halves

Melt butter or margarine in frying pan and cook onion about 5 minutes. Stir in the brown rice and cook for another minute. Add the chicken stock, lemon rind, water and salt and stir well. Bring to a boil, reduce the heat to low and cover the pan and simmer until the rice is tender and all the liquid is absorbed, about 35 minutes. Remove pan from heat and let stand 5 minutes with the lid on. Stir in the green onions, lemon juice and pecan halves.

PASTA WITH TOMATO AND LIME SAUCE

1 lb. of very ripe tomatoes, peeled and chopped
1 small bunch of tender young spinach
4 garlic cloves, crushed
½ lime grated rind
Juice of 2 limes
¼ tsp. chili sauce
12 oz. thin spaghetti (capellini)
2 tbsp. olive oil salt and pepper
Grated Parmesan cheese for serving

Combine tomatoes, spinach, garlic, lime rind, lime juice and chili sauce. Stir well to mix and set aside for about thirty minutes to blend the flavors. Cook pasta in boiling salted water just until tender. Drain and return to pan. Add the olive oil and tomato and lime sauce to the pasta. Season with salt and pepper. Add Parmesan cheese to taste, toss again and serve.

SALMON BAKE

½ whole salmon filet
2 tbsp. melted butter
1 lemon sliced
2 tbsp. fresh lemon juice

Set oven to 375 degrees. Place the salmon filet on a sheet of tin foil. Melt butter and add lemon juice. Pour over salmon and place lemon slices on top of salmon. Close the tin foil over the salmon making a package. Cook for 30 minutes in oven until fish flakes easily and is cooked through. Serve with fresh vegetables and a small salad.

LOW-FAT APPLE COBBLER

1 cup of instant oatmeal
¾ of a tin of frozen apple juice concentrate thawed
1 Golden delicious apple cut into bite-size pieces
¼ tsp. baking powder
1 cup whole wheat flour
1 egg
½ tsp. ground cinnamon
Non-stick cooking spray

Preheat oven to 350 degree F. Mix together all ingredients except the apples. Next, spoon ½ of the mixture into an 8" baking dish that has been sprayed with non-stick cooking spray. Top the mixture with the apples and drop by spoon the remaining mixture on top of the apples. Bake for 15-17 minutes.

PANCAKES WITH FRUIT

1 cup of pancake mix
1 cup of 2% milk
1 egg
1 fruit cup

Mix pancake mix, milk and egg together to make batter. Make pancakes on grill. Enjoy with a bowl of mixed fruit.

FRENCH TOAST

2 slices of whole-wheat bread
1 well beaten egg
¼ tsp. sugar
½ c. milk

Beat egg, sugar and milk together with a spoon. Dip bread slices in mixture and cook in fry pan that has been lightly sprayed with non-stick cooking spray. Top with your favorite fruit or low-fat jam.

HOME-MADE VEGETABLE SOUP

1 ½ lbs. lean ground beef
1 medium onion chopped fine
1 28 oz. can of diced tomatoes
2 cups water
3 cans of consommé
1 can tomato soup
4 carrots (grated or chopped fine)
1 bay leaf
3 sticks of celery (chopped fine)
parsley
pepper to taste
8 tbsps. of barley

Brown meat and onions in a frying pan. Drain off any fat. Combine all ingredients in a large pot and simmer, covered for at least 2 hours or all day. Serves 10.
This is a delicious meal and a nutritious after-school snack.

HEALTH BARS

Bottom Layer

2 tbsp. soft margarine
2 tbsp. brown sugar
1 tbsp. honey
1 tbsp. light molasses
1-cup quick rolled oats
2 tbsp. whole-wheat flour

Press into 8"x8"x2" square baking pan. Bake at 350 degrees for 5 minutes

While waiting for the bottom to bake pour ½ cup of boiling water and 1 tbsp. of margarine over 1 cup of mixed dried fruit pieces. Let stand for 5 minutes.

Add 1 slightly beaten egg or ¼ cup of eggbeaters, ¼ cup packed brown sugar, 1/4 cup of whole-wheat flour, 2 tbsp. wheat germ, 2 tbsp. wheat bran, ¾ tsp. cinnamon, ½ tsp. salt, ½ cup chopped walnuts. Stir together until well blended. Spread over pre-baked bottom crust. Return to 350-degree oven and bake for 25-30 minutes. Cool. Cut into squares.

TUNA BURGERS

1/3 cup of low-fat mayonnaise
½ tsp. salt
1.4 tsp. oregano
1 tbsp. minced onion
¼ cup tomato paste
¼ cup water
Grated parmesan cheese
1 7 oz. can solid tuna (in water) drained and broken up
4 whole-wheat hamburger buns

Preheat oven to 400 degrees F. Mix together mayo, salt, tuna, onion and oregano. Spread on bun halves. Blend tomato paste and water. Spoon over tuna mixture and sprinkle with grated parmesan cheese. Place on cookie sheet and bake for 10 minutes.

HEALTHY OATMEAL MUFFINS

1 cup of oatmeal
1 cup of buttermilk
1 cup of whole-wheat flour
1 tsp. baking powder
½ tsp. baking soda
½ tsp. salt
1 egg, beaten
4 tbsp. melted butter or margarine
½ cup raisins or snipped dates
Rind of 1 orange
1 cup of brown sugar

Pour buttermilk over oatmeal and let sit for 10 minutes. Combine flour, baking powder, soda, salt and brown sugar. Add beaten egg and butter and mix well. Pour in buttermilk mixture, add raisins and orange peel and bake at 400 degrees for 20 minutes in lined muffin tin.

LOW CALORIE VEGETABLE PLATTER

This is a good snack to have on hand. Keeps very well in the fridge and is the perfect food to reach for when those cravings hit.

1 or 2 heads of cauliflower
1 basket of cherry tomatoes
1 bunch of broccoli
3 to 4 carrots cut in small strips
1 bunch of chopped green onions
2 to 3 stalks of celery, sliced
1 can of button mushroom or fresh if available
1 tin pitted black olives, drained
1 8 oz. bottle of low-fat Italian dressing

Put all vegetables in a sealed plastic bowl. Pour Italian dressing over and marinate in the fridge for 24 hours, turning occasionally. Drain before serving on a platter.

5

...all those who have meditated on the art of governing mankind have been convinced that the fate of Empires depends on the education of youth...

—Aristotle

Journal Entry 9
Oct. 23, 1997

WANTED! The guy who stole my bag.

I don't know what it is. It seems like almost every few months I get something stolen. I'm like the guy who wears one of those big sombreros in the middle of crowd and no matter how much you try not to, your eyes are always automatically drawn to that guy. Well, I'm like that guy, singled out everywhere I go. My bag is gone and this time my jacket and my homework were in it. The teachers are going to believe that one alright. If people don't like me—FINE—but why the hell do they have to take my stuff? Just leave me alone! I feel like I'm some entertainment act for a show that never ends. Its bad enough I have little to no friends and I'm teased every waking moment. I feel like going away, hiding somewhere. I don't deserve this.

*Later that week I asked a friend if he knew anything about my bag. He said, "**no.**"*

Two weeks later that same friend was wearing my jacket. When I asked him about it he denied everything. That's what friends are for, right?

THE VITAMIN CONNECTION
(Before starting any diet or exercise program please consult your physician.)

WHAT ARE VITAMINS?

Vitamins are the substances found in the food we eat. In order for your body to function properly and grow you need to consume vitamins daily. There are two types of vitamins, fat-soluble and water-soluble.

Fat-soluble vitamins like Vitamin A, D, E and K are stored in the body until the body requires them. They can be stored from a few days up to a couple of weeks.

Water-soluble vitamins are vitamins that don't get stored in the body but travel through your bloodstream and your body collects what it needs and what ever it doesn't need, gets eliminated. Because these types of vitamins travel through your body, they need to be replaced often. These types of vitamins include Vitamin C, all the B vitamins, biotin and Pantothenic acid.

Your body has the ability to get the right amount and type of vitamins needed if you are eating a healthy diet. Taking a multivitamin is a great option if you're worried about getting enough vitamins in your diet.

Below is a list of supplements and vitamins that will help keep your body strong. These are found at your local health food store.

Antioxidants

Antioxidant vitamins such as E, C, and beta-carotene have potential healing capabilities e.g. lower cholesterol, fatty build-up in the arteries and reduce heart attack and stroke.

Beta Carotene

When taking beta carotene your body converts it into Vitamin A, a fat-soluble vitamin important for growth, reproduction and strengthening your immune system.

Food source for beta-carotene: e.g. Carrots, cantaloupe, tomatoes, pumpkin

Calcium

Calcium is a very important mineral to help keep your teeth and bones strong. It also helps nerve and muscle function.

Food Source for Calcium: e.g. Milk/skim milk, most dairy products, canned salmon and broccoli.

Flaxseed Oil

Flaxseed Oil contains the essential fatty acids Omega 3 and 6 (which are good fats) and help the function and structure of the brain and helps with memory, mood and concentration.

Food Source for Flaxseed Oil: e.g. Flaxseed Oil supplement or cereals with flaxseed.

Grape Seed

Grape Seed is a water-soluble vitamin that helps promote normal growth and development within the body. It helps with circulation and has a protective effect on the liver. It also helps varicose veins, swelling and bruising.

Food Source: Grape Seed supplement

Iron

Iron is a mineral and is very important in the transport of oxygen throughout the body.

Food Source: e.g. Found in all types of meat and whole grains, green, leafy vegetables such as spinach.

Magnesium

Magnesium is a mineral that helps your nerves and muscles function properly.

Food Source: e.g. Nuts, green veggies and whole grains.

Potassium

Potassium is a mineral that provides many functions through the body like maintaining electrical stability in the heart and nervous system. It also helps with cell grown and fluid balance.

Food Source: e.g. Fruits such as apples, bananas, cantaloupe, tomatoes, mushrooms beans and spinach.

Selenium

Selenium is an essential trace mineral in your body that helps with normal functioning of the immune system and your thyroid glands. It also helps control the levels of free radicals in your body that can damage cells.

Food Source: e.g. Some meats, seafood and bread plus brazil nuts and walnuts.

THE "B" VITAMIN FAMILY

Vitamin B3 (Niacin)

Vitamin B3 is important for energy and your metabolism. It can help lower bad cholesterol and raise good cholesterol levels in your body.
Food Source: Lean meats, fish, poultry, and peanut butter

Vitamin B6

Vitamin B6 plays an important role in helping you to maintain good health by helping build red blood cells and with the function of your nervous and immune system.
Food Source: e.g. Beans, fruit, veggies, poultry.

Vitamin B9 (Folic Acid)

Vitamin B9 is a water-soluble vitamin that helps keep with the formation of red blood cell formation and cell division. Folic Acid (B9) works great together with B6 and B12 to help reduce health risks.
Food Source: e.g. Juices, fruits, liver, dark veggies, bread, pasta, rice.

Vitamin B12

Vitamin B12 is good for maintaining healthy red blood cells and nerve cells. It also helps to build the genetic materials in all cells.
Food Source: e.g. Animal foods, fish, milk, eggs, poultry.

Vitamin A

Vitamin A is a fat-soluble vitamin that helps promote healthy vision, a healthy immune system and can help fight infections.
Food Source: e.g. Milk, eggs, chicken, dark green veggies, oranges, carrots, cantaloupe, tomatoes or tomato juice.

Vitamin C

Vitamin C is a water-soluble vitamin that helps promote growth and development. It also helps the body's immune system and promotes the healing of wounds. It is also good for your teeth and gums.
Food Source: e.g. Citrus fruits, strawberries, cantaloupe, green veggies.

Vitamin D

Vitamin D is a fat-soluble vitamin. Vitamin D's plays a major role in maintaining strong bones in the body. A good way to get Vitamin D is to spend time outside in the sun (make sure you wear a sunscreen though).
Food Source: e.g. fortified foods. Look for Vitamin D in milk and milk products.

Vitamin E

Vitamin E is an antioxidant that protects the body tissues from damage of oxidation. It helps in the formation of red blood cells.
Food Source: e.g. Nuts, olives, asparagus, leafy greens.

Vitamin Supplements to Consider:

Whether you have diabetes or not vitamin supplements can be a good choice. Foods rich in Vitamin B6, riboflavin, calcium, zinc, folic acid, coenzyme Q10 and amino acids are beneficial. Using flaxseed, safflower, canola, olive or soybean oil is a good choice for cooking and/or salads.

The above is just a brief outline of the vitamins and minerals that are available to help you promote good health. If you are interested in information on vitamins and minerals and meal replacement shakes, protein shakes and protein bars, visit your local health food store where there are brochures available on this subject.

6

...to climb steep hills requires a slow pace at first...

—*Shakespeare*

Journal Entry 8
October 19, 1997

"LOVE STINKS"

For three years now, ever since grade 8, I have liked this girl so much that every time I see her the butterflies in my stomach are so strong that I feel like I'm going to throw up.

The sad thing is I don't know if she even knows me. I'm sure she has seen me before, who hasn't; I'm like Jabba the Hut walking down the hall. People part like the Red Sea when I pass by. For three years I have been trying to muster up the courage just to talk to her. I'm so nervous but I think I'm going to try to talk to her and if it goes good maybe I'll ask her out.

I left class to go to the bathroom and to my surprise she was walking down the hall at the same time. I was so scared, that as she got closer, my heart felt like it was going to jump out of my chest and take off down the hall. I could feel my face turning red like I was going to have a heart attack but I said to myself, "I can do this." So as she got closer I said, Hey how's it going?" stuttering like a fool. She looked at me and smiled and laughing said "not too bad, you?" I froze like a deer in the head lights. The shock of hearing her sweet voice answer back was too much. I was about to say something but all of a sudden her friends came out of nowhere. One of them said," Why the hell you talking to him?" "Watch out he might take a bite out of you!" My chance of talking to her was gone and it wasn't just that she had joined in their laughter, but as she looked at me right in the eye, I was overwhelmed by such a feeling of sadness. The courage it had taken me three long years to find had disappeared in just a few moments and once again I was being laughed at.

Getting beat up would have been easy compared to being laughed at by someone you liked for so long. Her loss!

(Before starting any diet or exercise program please consult your physician.)

You have learned many new things so far and now it's time to turn yourself into that new self-image that you have locked in your mind. Now that you know how to make goals, create a new positive attitude, develop the will power and mind power to block out negativity around you and have your new diet plan and new self-image mapped out and locked in your mind, you are finally ready to put all your new skills to work and get yourself in the GYM. It's time to exercise! This is the fun part. You will be seeing your body transform into the new image you have visualized for yourself. Don't get discouraged. This is what you have always wanted. It's time to walk that path to success. You can do it! I believe in you—now YOU believe in yourself.

There will be 3 stages to the program, Beginners, Intermediate and Advanced. These stages will help show you your progress and tell you where to start and when to move on. These are your blueprints for building a better body. The Beginners Program is where most of you will start. This part of the program will help show you the proper methods and techniques to start your training and will act as the foundation, the strength, upon which your other building blocks will fit.

It is important for you to engage in both aerobic and non-aerobic exercises. Aerobic exercises are all types of cardiovascular activity, for example, walking, running, biking, playing sports. The benefits of aerobic exercise is to help build your cardiovascular system, increase your heart rate and intake of oxygen as well as help your body burn off calories in order to lose weight. Non-aerobic activity such as weight training helps your body to build muscle and tone up. With the combination of both aerobic and non-aerobic exercises, your body will not just lose weight and tone up much quicker and become healthier, but exercise also helps to lower blood pressure, balance out sugar and insulin levels, as well as help reduce major health problems you might endure later in life (i.e. Diabetes, Heart Disease, Cancer, etc.).

Level of Intensity

Intensity plays a major role in getting your body to burn more fat. No matter what level of fitness you are it's always important to start out slow and build your way up. Your heart, being a muscle, needs to be worked like any other muscle in order for it to stay strong. Walking at a stroll or low intensity level for 50 min. does not have the same beneficial results as a 25 min. speed walk at a higher intensity level. Even though the 50 min. walk is double the time the level of intensity is a little higher in the 25 min. speed walk, therefore, you burned off more calories in half the time. In order to know if you are in a good aerobic fat burning zone your body should be sweating, you should have good color in your face, be somewhat short of breath to a point where you can talk but in short sentences and not long conversations, and have a feeling that you are working yourself. While doing long but low intensity cardio is still good for you, it is not the most beneficial way to spend your time at the gym if you want to see results sooner. The key (when you are feeling comfortable and at your own personal pace) is to lower the time doing an exercise and up the intensity so you can bring yourself to the point where your body feels the workout and you begin to experience the effects mentioned above. Besides increasing the speed that you walk, run, bike, or play you can always try elevating your treadmill to a higher incline or bike up some hills on the stationary bike. This will help put you at that level of intensity to achieve your goal. Use your imagination and experiment with different ways to make your workouts fun and beneficial to your health.

Types of Cardio

When you start looking for challenges and become more physically fit it's important that you alternate your cardio workout. Never try doing the same routine all the time because your body will start to adapt to it and you will not get the results you're looking for. Keep your mind and body excited about going to the gym and look forward to trying different exercises and routines. Remember, you can add your workout routines to your affirmation cards to help accomplish your goals. Below are some types of cardio you can try.

Walking

Walking is a great form of exercise. You can do it anywhere, it doesn't cost you anything but the benefits are priceless. Take advantage of the opportunity to exercise your body by walking to school, walking to the store or a friend's house. If this is not possible use the treadmill at school or the gym whenever you can. Walking is the best cardio workout for anyone who has not exercised in a while and is just starting out on a new exercise program. To receive the best results for effective weight loss, speed and incline play a major role in walking. Remember to set the right level of intensity for yourself. You want to feel comfortable, but remember, this isn't a walk in the park. To gain the best results and grow stronger, you have to begin to push yourself a little harder each time.

Bicycling

Bicycling is a great way to help lose weight. It boosts the intensity of your workout and gets your heart rate going. This exercise is easy on the joints and the results are great when you incorporate hills in your routine. Also, this is another exercise to take advantage of if you can't get to the gym. Remember, you can always bike to school, the store, or anywhere—take advantage of it.

Running

Running is more challenging than walking and it's not for everyone. If you have any knee or joint problems running might not be for you. To know when your ready to run is simple, if you can walk for a good 30 to 40 minutes without stopping then you can probably try running. Start by walking for 5 minutes then go to a light jog for 3 to 5 minutes then go back to a walk for another 5 minutes. Repeat the walk and jog for about 15 to 20 min. After doing that routine a few times you can try warming up and going right into a jog/run for about 15minutes without resting and work your way up from there. You can always experiment with the speed and incline levels to help keep your intensity level up. Remember, don't just use the treadmill for running instead take advantage of your surroundings by running to school, to work, to the store. You will be amazed at how energetic you will feel!

Swimming

Swimming is ideal for people that have knee or joint problems or if you have a lot of weight to lose. When you're swimming, the water supports you by not putting any strain on your body and joints. Besides just swimming, try out water aerobics to help benefit your workout. Remember, don't be shy about swimming like I once was. Negativity doesn't get you down anymore so use the skills that I have taught you (Chapter 2) and don't let anyone bully or tease you if you want to go swimming. You can do anything now!

Elliptical Machines

The Elliptical machine trainer is a great source of cardio with a low impact motion. It's great for people that enjoy running without the impact on the lower back and knees. Most models do offer some kind of resistance program to help increase your intensity.

Rowing/Rowing Machines

Rowing is a great outdoor activity and cardio machine in the gym. If your community offers a rowing team or a program "GO FOR IT!!" Don't be shy about joining teams, it's a great way to make friends and lose weight. Rowing is a great exercise for your core muscles and arms and helps build up a great cardiovascular system.

Stair Climber Machine

Stair climbers provide a great aerobic workout but it's also not for everyone and should be used carefully. If you have any lower body problems or injuries I recommend not using the stair climber. The stair climber is an easy machine to cheat on by letting the pedals bounce off the ground or not stepping low enough. I recommend speaking to an instructor at your gym or wherever you are using the machine to find out the proper way of operating it. When done properly it provides one of the best cardio workouts.

Group/Team Aerobics

The key, along with your new outlook on life, is being as active as you can. Joining teams or groups is one of the best things you can do for yourself by getting out there and making new friends and being active. In order to be that new person, you must try new things. Remember, try not to be shy or scared about joining a team or group activities. Use the methods I have gone over with you and you'll do great. Concentrate and focus on the activity and yourself. If there is negativity around you don't be scared. Block that negativity out with your positive thinking and just keeping believing in yourself and do the things you have always wanted to do.

Weight Training

Weight training is a key aspect in your fitness program. It helps harden, strengthen, and tone your body plus improves your athletic abilities. When first starting your weight training it might seem intimidating but don't let that get you down or scare you away. Use your Affirmation Cards and visualization skills to remind yourself not to get intimidated by the weights. Remind yourself that this is fun and easy and you will benefit from starting out slow. Like any exercise you need to start out slow and move your way up to help prevent soreness, injury and becoming discouraged. Through the Beginners, Intermediate, and Advanced Programs I have put together for you, it will help show you the best way to start out and move forward in your workout routines. With the combination of both aerobic and weight training exercises you will be able to receive the best results for getting into shape.

Feeling the Exercise

When entering the gym it is always important to start out with a light aerobic (5 minute) warm up and a stretch. When starting your first few sets of exercises you may feel a little discomfort in your muscles and joints. This is just your body preparing itself for weight training so don't let this scare you, the discomfort should go away after a few sets.

For the remainder of your workout you can experience a weird or strange feeling in the middle or belly of the muscles that you are working. This is a good sign. This means your working the muscle and that's good. The charts below will help show where and where not to feel the exercise.

Exercise	*Right Place*	*Wrong Place*
• Bicep curl	Upper Arm	Elbows, Wrists
• Lat Pull down	Upper Back	Shoulder Joints, Arms
• Bench Press	Chest, Triceps	Shoulder Joints
• Abdominal sit-ups	Midsection	Lower Back, Neck
• Shoulder Press	Shoulder, Upper back	Elbows, Neck
• Seated Row	Mid-Back	Lower Back, Arms
• Triceps extension	Back Upper Arm	Elbows
• Leg Curl	Hamstrings	Lower Back, Gluteus
• Leg Extension	Quadriceps	Knees
• Squats	Thighs, Gluteus	Knees, Lower Back

What is Over Training

Although we sometimes like to believe that we are invincible the truth is that we are not. Everybody's body has limits and over training your body seems to come in many different forms. For instance, sneaking in a few more exercises into your routine or even over doing an exercise may leave your body in a state in which you lack any energy for a few days or weeks to come. Over doing it may even weaken your immune system leaving you vulnerable to a cold or flu. There are several ways in which over training can manifest itself but the important thing is to remember that fitness is achieved through a combination of exercise, resting and recovery, not just exercise alone. So keep your mind on the path to success, have patience and sooner or later your goals will be accomplished.

Stretching

Stretching before any activity is well worth your time. It helps increase the flow of oxygen, nutrients and blood to the muscles in your body. It also enhances an athlete's physical fitness, increases relaxation, range of motion, helps reduce stress, muscle soreness and helps prevent injuries. Before beginning your stretch follow these guidelines:

- *Warm up to increase blood flow and body temperature to active muscles*
- *Isolate each muscle group to be stretched*
- *Move slowly and smoothly into each stretch*
- *Breath normally and freely while stretching*
- *Hold each stretch for 20 seconds to 1 min. then relax*
- ***Do not strain or force*** *your muscles beyond its normal range of motion*
- *Concentrate and feel the stretch*
- *Come in and out of each stretch slowly*
- *After any activity remember to stretch again*

The following are some basic stretches you can try:

Workout Chart

Keeping a chart of what you do and how you do it is very important in moving forward with your training and completing your goals. By keeping track of your constant improvements it helps you see what works for you and what does not. It will help keep your goals on track and up to date plus by charting your progress and seeing your improvements on paper, it will help create better visualization skills which, in turn, develop better results and self-image in your subconscious. In each level, (Beginners, Intermediate, and Advanced), there will be workout charts for you to write down your results and see your progress to help you determine when you are ready to move to the next level.

No Access to a Gym

If you are too young or you have no access to a gym, "don't worry." The key aspect is to follow the methods that I have taught you throughout the book and to concentrate on only aerobic activities. For example, take advantage of your surroundings by running around the block, running to school or wherever you feel comfortable. You can also enhance your aerobic program by using a bicycle or roller blades. Try to start doing as much activity as you can. When you can't get to the gym to do any non-aerobic (weight lifting) exercises, start doing sit-ups and push-ups at home to help strengthen and tone your body.

BEGINNERS PROGRAM

The Beginners Program is the introduction for transforming your body into the new self-image you have seen in your mind. The program consists of aerobic exercises and 14 non-aerobic weightlifting exercises that will help introduce your body to physical fitness. The program covers a 4-week period and by the end of the fourth week you should be able to move on to the next level. At the Beginners level, all exercises in this program are made to start out slow and let your body get used to exercise. The following list shows you the non-aerobic/weight training exercises you are going to be learning in the Beginners Program and the proper way to do them.

Note: *For the Beginners Program, pick a light weight that you can lift 12-15 times. Your 12th-15th repetition should be challenging but not impossible. Do two to three sets of each exercise. Be sure to rest for 60 seconds in between sets. When using weights, it is advisable to have a friend or parent there to spot or assist you.*

Bench Press

Lying flat on the bench, start by grabbing the barbell with a wide grip and lower the bar to your chest or slightly above it. Then, press upward until your arms are extended and then repeat.

Sets—2-3
Reps.—12-15

Incline Press

Set bench at a 30-degree angle. Grab a pair of dumbbells, sit on the bench and lift them up to your ears with your palms facing forward and your elbows bent at a 90-degree angle. Press the dumbbells over your head with a slight arch until your arms are fully extended. Slowly return to the start position and repeat.

Sets—2-3
Reps.—12-15

Machine Fly

Adjust the seat so that you are able to lock your arms in the proper position on the machine. Move slowly through the entire movement and contract and squeeze your chest muscles. Slowly return to starting position and repeat.

Sets—2-3
Reps.—12-15

Press Down (Triceps)

Stand 1 ft. away from the cable stack and grasp the bar with a shoulder-wide over-hand grip. Keep your back straight and your knees bent slightly. Place and tuck your elbows into your sides. Extend your arms downward keeping your elbows tucked in and not bending your wrists. Return to starting position and repeat.

Sets—2-3
Reps.—12-15

Leg Extension Machine

Sit on the machine so that your back lies against the support and your feet fit snugly under the pads. Hold handles for support and straighten your legs so that they are parallel to the floor. Return to starting position and repeat.

Sets—2-3
Reps.—12-15

Leg Curl Machine

Depending on the machine, stand or sit so that the pads fit comfortable on the back of your legs. Curl your legs so that they are at a 90-degree angle. Release and then repeat.

Sets—2-3
Reps.—12-15

Abdominal Crunch

Lying on your back bring your knees up
leaving your feet flat on the floor. Tuck in
your stomach so your back is flat against
the floor and slowly begin lifting your shoulders off the floor as far as you can until you
begin to feel your stomach contract.

Sets—2-3
Reps—20

Lat Pull-down

Adjust seat pad so it rests comfortably on
your thighs once you are in a sitting position. The bar should be just over your head.
Grab it with a wide grip with your back
arched slightly. Pull the bar down to your
collarbone bringing your elbows back and
squeezing your shoulder blades together.
Return to starting position and repeat.

Sets—2-3
Reps. 12-15

A Seated Row

Sit with your knees slightly bent and grab
the bar. Keeping your back straight, pull
and squeeze the bar towards your lower
chest. Try not to lean back. Return to starting position and repeat.

Sets—2-3
Reps.—12-15

Shoulder Fly—Front/Side

Standing with your feet shoulder width apart and your knees slightly bent, grab a pair of dumbbells and stand with your arms at your side. Keep your elbows slightly bent, not locked, and extend your arms out beside you, and then back down to your sides. Repeat.

Sets—2-3
Reps.—12-15

Then standing in the same position, extend your arms out in front of you, one at a time, and lower back down again.

Dumbbell Curl

Standing with your feet shoulder width apart and your knees slightly bent, grab a pair of dumbbells and stand with your arms at your side. As you curl the dumbbell, rotate your wrist so that your palm is facing upward at the top of the curl then return to starting position turning your palm back to your side as it was in the starting position. Repeat.

Sets—2-3
Reps. 12-15

Cable Curl

Standing a foot away from the cable stack
set the bar to the lowest level. Grab bar
with an underhand grip, tuck elbows into
your sides and curl bar up toward your
chest. Slowly bring bar back down to starting position. Repeat.

Sets—2-3
Reps.—12-15

Sit-up Ball Crunch

Sit on top of exercise ball with your legs in
front of you, feet flat on the floor and hands
by your ears. Keeping your feet flat on the
floor, slowly lean back and roll yourself
along the ball until your torso is parallel to
the floor. Next, slowly curl yourself up letting your shoulders and upper back lift off
the ball. Repeat.

Sets—2-3
Reps.—12-15

Decline Press

Straddle the decline bench. Lay back and
grab the bar with a wide grip. Slowly lift and
bring down the bar so that it is just above
your chest and press until your arms are
extended. Repeat.

Sets 2-3
Reps. 10-12

When entering the gym to start your workout or if you are starting your workout at home, remember to follow these guidelines.

Guidelines

- Start with a 5-10 minute warm-up

- Do a full body stretch

- Start with your non-aerobic (weight training) exercises first

- Now do your aerobic activity for 10-20 minutes and work your way up. Being new, start out slow but maintain a good intensity level.

- End with a cool down and another full body stretch.

Note: *For those who don't have access to a gym, follow the same guidelines but for the non-aerobic exercises, remember to try doing some push ups and sit ups and concentrate more on your aerobic activity.*

Suggestion*: If possible, get some resistance bands to help you with your non-aerobic exercises. They are portable and can be taken with you anywhere, even on holidays.*

Remember to follow the guidelines before and after your workouts. Also try different aerobic activities each week to find the ones that you like most. Continue following the techniques I have shown you throughout the book and you will do great!

INTERMEDIATE PROGRAM

Now that you have already been a month into your workout program you should be ready to up the intensity and begin the Intermediate Program. If you feel that you are not ready to proceed to the next level, keep working out at the Beginners level until you feel comfortable enough to move on. The Intermediate Program will consist of some of the same non-aerobic weight lifting exercises along with some new ones that I have added. In this part of the program you are going to concentrate on lifting a little more weight and increasing the intensity and time spent doing your aerobic exercises. By now you should be seeing some result in your overall physical fitness and your energy level. Keep up the positive outlook and skills you have learned in the book along with your *New Healthy Diet* and you will feel great.

Below are the new non-aerobic weight-lifting exercises that you are going to add to your routine.

Barbell Squat

Stand with the bar resting across your traps and shoulder, your feet flat, shoulder-width apart. Bend your knees and drop your hips back and down, descending until your thighs are parallel to the floor or slightly lower. Keep your back straight. Return to starting position. Repeat.

Sets—2-3
Reps.—10-12

Bent-over Barbell Row

Position yourself over the barbell with your feet planted firmly on the floor. Bend at the waist keeping your back straight. Grasp the bar with both hands and raise the weight off the floor. Keeping your back flat, but angled, pull your elbows behind your back as far as you can without the bar touching your stomach. Lower to starting position. Repeat.

Sets—2-3
Reps.—10-12

Rope Extension

Stand 1 ft. away from the cable stack. Set rope to the highest level. Grab the rope, keeping your elbows tucked into your sides and extend your arms downwards contracting your triceps. Bring your arms slowly back to the starting position. Repeat.

Sets—2-3
Reps.—10-12

Incline Curl

Lie on and adjust bench to a 65-degree angle. Hold a pair of dumbbells at arms length. Curl dumbbell and twist your wrist so that your palms are facing upward. Keep your elbows locked and your upper arms should not move at all. Slowly lower your arms to starting position. Repeat.

Sets—2-3
Reps.—10-12

Intermediate Guidelines

- Start with a 5-10 minute warm-up

- Have a full body stretch

- Start with your non-aerobic weight training exercises (pick a weight you can lift 10-12 times). The 10th or 12th repetition should be challenging but not impossible. Do two to three sets of each exercise resting 1 minute in between sets.

- Do your aerobic activity. Being in the Intermediate stage, start out at a good pace and proceed into a higher intensity level. Do at least 20-30 minutes of aerobic activity.

- Do a 5 minute cool down

- End with a full body stretch

Follow the guidelines and remember to try different aerobic activities to give your body a challenge.

ADVANCED PROGRAM

You are now two months into your workout. You should be feeling great and noticing huge changes in your body. You should feel ready to move on to the Advanced Program. If you're not ready, there's no rush. Keep up the good work and proceed when you feel ready.

In the Advanced Program we are going to concentrate on intensity and increasing your workout and taking it to a higher level. There will be a few non-aerobic exercises to try and an increase in the aerobic activity.

We are going to increase the intensity be decreasing the rest time between exercises and making your workout more like a "circuit training program."

Circuit Training Program

I have broken down the exercises into two groups of 3 exercises each. These groups of 3 exercises are performed without any break between the sets. You will do 3 sets of each group, resting 2 minutes in between each set. Example:

Group # 1—Bench Press, Cable Fly, Decline Press x 3 sets (rest 2 minutes)

Group # 2—Overhead Press, Press-down, Squats x 3 sets (rest 2 minutes).

Finish one group of exercises before moving on to the next group. After finishing your groups of non-aerobic exercises proceed to the aerobic part of your program. Do a 25-40 minute aerobic activity at a high intensity level (you can vary the intensity levels during your 25-40 minute aerobic exercise).

Below are the new non-aerobic exercises that you will now add to your routine.

Cable Fly

Standing in the middle of the cable stacks,
set pulleys to a high level. Extend both
arms and grab the handles. With your back
straight and your knees slightly bent press
the cables down and forward in front of
your chest keeping your elbows slightly
bent. Slowly return to starting position.
Repeat.

Sets—2-3
Reps.—10-12

Overhead Press

With your back to the cable stack, set rope
to a high level. Reach back and grab the
rope, taking one step forward and leaning
forward with your elbows tucked in close to
your head, extend your arms forward contracting your triceps. Slowly bring back so
the rope is right above your head.
Repeat.

Sets—2-3
Reps.—10-12

Rope Crunch

Kneel in front of a cable stack holding a
rope handle attached to a high pulley. Pull
your sternum contracting your abs down
toward your pelvis while rounding your
back. Return to starting position. Repeat.

Sets—2-3
Reps.—20

Advanced Program Guidelines

- Start with a 5-10 minute warm-up.

- Full body stretch

- Start with your non-aerobic circuit training exercises (follow the circuit training guideline)

- Do your aerobic activity. Being at the advanced stage start with a good pace and do high intensity intervals over a period of 25-40 minutes.

- End with a cool down and a full body stretch.

Now that you are at the Advanced Program level continue with this Program and add new exercises at your own pace. After the 4 weeks, continue with your training. Exercising and eating healthy, nutritious foods will now have become part of your life. As each day goes by you are experiencing the positive effects of your hard work. You have greater self-esteem, more confidence, a toned and healthy body. You are in control so continue on the path to success and never give up. You have developed the skills to move on and maintain a healthy lifestyle. Keep up the good work and apply what you have learned to all aspects of your life.

YOUR FUTURE

Changing your life by adapting a healthy, new lifestyle and seeing the benefits that positive thinking can create and the way you now look at life is fantastic. Whether it was to lose weight, eliminate bullying from your life or just wanting to improve your outlook, I want to congratulate you and wish you good luck in all your future endeavors. The techniques and skills you have learned while reading *EPIDEMIC, A Survivor's Story* have now become a part of you and can be recalled to address any situation that may confront you in the future.

My success did not stop after I graduated from high school. By continuing with my training and using the visualization techniques I have outlined in the book I believe I have created a strong foundation for myself on which to build my future. I continue to say ***"whatever I want to be, I will be and there is nothing that can stop me."*** By using these same techniques I know you can reach the goals you set for yourself too.

I have dreams and goals that I am always setting for myself. I would love to play in the NBA (I did become a great 3-point shooter by using my visualization skills) and acting has always been something I was interested in but on the road to my own self-discovery I feel I have other missions to accomplish. At twenty-two I have written *EPIDEMIC, A Survivor's Story* with the hope of helping millions of young kids and adults learn from it and positively change their lives forever. It is also my goal to develop youth centers for young kids that suffer from obesity, bullying and other problems. I have many more goals which I look forward to facing and accomplishing in the near future. Always realize that you can refer back to this book at any age for any problem, at any time in your life. I wish nothing but the best for you.

<u>CONCLUSION</u>

I am on a mission to rid obesity, bullying, harassment and negativity from the lives of young people. Through my book I plan to accomplish this mission.

It is my hope that as a society who treasures their young people, we can begin to realize that so many are suffering in silence, and that by working together, we can begin to eliminate this epidemic.

Everyone has a dream and my dream was to write this book and help those who suffer from this epidemic like I once did. I believe my book holds the key to your future by bettering your life, giving you hope, teaching you to have a positive outlook on life and to make your dreams become a reality by showing you the path to success. *"EPIDEMIC, A Survivor's Story"* was written to expose this epidemic that is haunting young people today. By showing young people how to take control of their lives through a positive attitude, visualization and meditation they will realize that it is **"in your mind"** where the answer lies; <u>**NOT**</u> in some magic pill or drink or drastic surgery. In your mind is where I have taught you to block out the negativity that torments you and to love life by showing you how to develop a positive mind set, a strong self-esteem, a strong self-image and the willpower to conquer your fears and put you on that path to success.

What you have read throughout my book is the answer you have been looking for. Together we are going to accomplish what you only thought was a dream but now will become your reality. Don't miss seeing how beautiful the world is by walking with your head down. It's now time to see how beautiful life and the world really is. Raise that head up high, the world is waiting for you!

....greatness is not in where we stand but in what direction we are moving. We must sail sometimes with the wind and sometimes against it but sail we must and not drift, nor lie anchor—Oliver Wendell Holmes—

978-0-595-67586-9
0-595-67586-7

Printed in the United States
64481LVS00004B/10-27

9 780595 675869